Backpacking
Hijinks

DENNIS MUELLER

NEWMAN SPRINGS PUBLISHING
320 Broad Street
Red Bank, NJ 07701

First originally published by Newman Springs Publishing 2019

ISBN 978-1-64531-186-7 (Paperback)
ISBN 978-1-64531-187-4 (Digital)

Printed in the United States of America

Contents

Acknowledgments

This book is dedicated to two key people in my backpacking life, my friend and backpacking partner, John, and the other is my drafting teacher from high school, Mr. B. All the names except John and Mr. B mentioned in this book have been changed to protect my friends from any embarrassment and to protect me from getting in trouble for ratting them out.

For over twenty-five years John was my partner in crime while backpacking and, more importantly, a good friend I trusted to have my back while hiking in the High Sierra's of northern California and other locations. Almost every year John and I would plan our seven- to ten-day backpacking trips, and almost every year I would bounce an idea for a crazy practical joke off of him to see what he thought. John took an active part in many of the jokes I planned. He was who I would ask for help with either developing the joke or in the delivery of them, and he always had a very calm demeanor about him. It was his demeanor and casual or laidback attitude that made him so believable when he was telling a story that supported a practical joke. He was so casual and laidback, he earned the nickname of Casual John from a lot of his friends.

As for Mr. B, he was probably the most influential person in my backpacking saga. It was Mr. B who introduced me to backpacking in the summer of 1983, and it was Mr. B who encouraged me to write this book. Every year when I returned from one of my adventures, I'd sit down with Mr. B and tell him what we saw, what we did, and I always told him what kind of a joke or two I played on my backpacking friends.

These two guys, along with all my friends who trusted me enough to take them on outdoor backpacking adventures, are the main reason I have continued thirty years of back country adventures, and hope to continue hiking in the woods for many more to come.

Introduction

When I was a young boy, my mom and dad would take me and my brothers camping. Sometimes we would take our neighborhood friends with us, but most of the time it was just our family. My parents would sleep in a camper while my four brothers and I would sleep in tents outside. My dad loved the back country of Northern California, specifically the areas near Mammoth Lakes, California. Often while camping he would teach us useful things related to the outdoors, but sometimes he would play silly practical jokes on us too.

Later on in my teenage years, I would go camping with other friends and they too would play jokes on me. Like the good ole' "Snipe Hunt" where they drug me out at night over a creek or two just to leave me in the dark without a flashlight trying to catch the infamous "Snipe," and later try to figure out how to get back to camp without falling in the creeks we crossed earlier using a flashlight. There was also the rubber snake in the sleeping bag trick that was played on me a couple of times, and to this day I still check my sleeping bag for mysterious critters when camping.

Almost all of my camping experience was with my mom and dad. Often we would head down a dirt road deep into the forest and find a spot near a mountain stream. My dad always seemed to know where to go, and then set up camp. We did this for several years while I was a kid, but when I was about sixteen years old, my parents got a divorce and my camping days ended. It wasn't until after high school when I was on my own that I started to explore the great outdoors once again.

During my high school years, Mr. B, who was my high school drafting teacher, kept asking me if I would like to join him and some other guys on his annual backpacking trip in the High Sierra Mountains of northern California. The area he liked to hike was a very remote area north of Yosemite and off the beaten path of most backpackers. At the end of the school year Mr. B would ask if I'd like to join him, and every year I had to turn him down due to other obligations I had and the fact I didn't have the cash to pay for the equipment nor the time off from work. However, it was the summer of 1983, five years after I graduated high school, when I finally had the chance, the cash, and the opportunity to join him; not to mention it was the year I was getting married and I thought once I'm married I wouldn't get the chance to ever go again. Boy was I wrong, for the next thirty-five years I was able to go backpacking and explore the great outdoors with my friends and introduce many of them to the joys of backpacking. One of the joys I had was taking new people out backpacking and showing them the beauty of the remote lakes, canyons, rivers, and breathtaking views, not to mention playing innocent practical jokes on my friends too. I even enjoyed the practical jokes that were played on me.

The practical jokes which I played were never meant to cause harm to anyone, nor to make fun of anyone either. The jokes were developed and played out to make the backpacking experience more memorable than just slapping on a backpack and go out camping in the mountains for a week or so. It was the jokes that made everyone laugh, not at each other, but about the journey the joke took them on. Some jokes took days to play out, while others were played in minutes. Each time a joke was played and revealed to the person who was on the receiving end, the joke took on its own life and added a new story to be told. We would all laugh, but more importantly, the people felt appreciated knowing we would spend a lot of time and effort developing the joke specifically for them. I am pleased to say that everyone who has ever gone on a backpacking trip with John and me are still our friends today.

This book is not solely about a variety of practical jokes which were played in the mountains, but more importantly a book full of fun stories and adventures, which I hope others will enjoy. I hope those who read this book will enjoy the true stories and maybe take it upon themselves to improve the jokes and share their stories with others as they too enjoy spending time with their friends in the great outdoors.

Chapter 1

Understanding the Terrain
and Campsites

(This chapter contains no practical jokes, only a description of the campsites and some of the terrain.)

The stories and practical jokes in this book were carried out hundreds of miles away from my home, deep in the mountainous area of the High Sierras just north of Yosemite National Park and other regions in the north western part of the United States. With this in mind, if a joke required a specific item to make the gag work, no matter what the size or weight, it had to be hidden in a backpack, driven over twelve hours or more and then carried the entire route to one of the main camps. Sometimes these items added several pounds to my pack, but in the end it was well worth the effort.

In order to appreciate the effort needed to play some of the practical jokes told in this book, one must gain a good sense of the terrain, the distances traveled carrying our backpacks, and an understanding of the locations where most of these jokes were played. There were three main campsites which were developed over the years where John and I hiked. It was at these three sites, and along the trails to them, where many of the practical jokes were played out and laughed about for years to follow. The camps are known to us as Base Camp 1, Base Camp 2, and Camp 3.

Base Camp 1

After driving for twelve hours the day before we hiked to Base Camp 1, we would get back into our cars and head out to the trailhead the following morning. We would then drive another twenty miles, four of which is down a dirt forestry road to an established trailhead where we could park our cars. Once at the trailhead, we would grudgingly struggle to get our forty- to fifty-pound backpacks on our backs and start hiking.

Base Camp 1 was an awesome spot to camp and was discovered by Mr. B several decades before I ever set foot on it. The only problem with Base Camp 1 was the difficulty getting to it, and it typically took about eight hours of hiking at a fairly steady pace to reach it. Sometimes it would take us two days to get there depending on who was in our group.

The hike starts out on a fairly established trail which leads you up and down a variety of mountain sides, past a couple of creeks, lakes, and other trails that lead off to a variety of other destinations, many of which John and I have explored over the past thirty-five years. Most of the trail is very dusty because of the amount of foot traffic and the lack of rain during the end of July when John and I typically would plan our trips.

For the next several hours the guys who hiked with us would constantly ask, "Are we there yet?" and John or I would always say, "It's around the next bend," which it wasn't. They soon learned not to ask us that question anymore and would hope we would get there soon. We would hike up one mountain, then down another, only to find there was a river to cross, a ridge to climb, and everything else but flat land. One part of the trail is up a 900-foot-high cliff where the trail switches back and forth until you reach the top. At the top is a beautiful mountain lake where we would typically stop to take a break or maybe even a swim before heading off again. The locals called the switch backs the "Golden Staircase," but most of the guys who hiked with me called it something else.

The first ten or twelve miles were on a designated trail leading to the granite, and I mean granite as far as the eye can see. Once we hit the granite, we got off the trail and headed to Base Camp 1, which was another four to five miles away. In order to reach Base Camp 1 we had to hike down this granite mountain side, which was so steep we had to zigzag back and forth down the mountain at a slow pace or risk the chance of falling and rolling to our death. Most of the guys called this mountain "Cardiac Hill" because of the amount of stress it put on our bodies and minds when either climbing down it or back up this mountain of granite. One guy almost lost all of his toenails because of the pressure he was placing on his toes trying to walk down the mountain. It wasn't a fun hike down, but once you got down the mountain, Base Camp 1 was there waiting for you.

Once at Base Camp 1 we would typically stay there for two to three days. While at this location we would go on a couple of day hikes to various lakes in the area or rest a day or so before heading deeper into the mountains. Base Camp 1 is about 6,500 feet above sea level and was surrounded by huge granite mountains that towered all around the camp. To the east is a valley which looks like it was formed by two granite mountain ranges that bumped into each other in a very violent manner. The mountains were massive in size and each had a very rugged form to them. At the base of these mountains was a valley with a river flowing down it toward the camp. The river is about fifteen feet wide in most areas but wider in others. Along the river's route down the valley, meadows formed, rocky areas with white water had been created, and in several locations large pools of water can be found, which are great for fishing or swimming. Also along the way are spattering of pine trees and bushes typically found along most mountain rivers.

As the river continues down the valley, it flows right by Base Camp 1 where it forms a huge swimming and fishing hole before it continues past the camp on further off to the west where it disappears among a small group of tall pine trees and mountains to the west.

To the south, just across the river from Base Camp 1, was another huge granite mountain range which ran along the river from east to west. This mountain range stood at least 1,000 feet above our campsite. And to the north were other granite mountains and cliffs that rose hundreds if not thousands of feet into the air above our camp. All the granite mountains around Base Camp 1 had a few trees here and there scattered along the sides and tops of them, but most were these huge canvases of granite as far as the eye could see.

Many of the granite cliffs and mountains which surrounded the camp have deep dark stains etched into them where water would run off them during storms and spring thaws. At the base of these mountains and specifically in Base Camp 1 is a fairly large area of semi-flat terrain, which boarders the main river, which flows through camp and a smaller stream, which flows down from a mountain lake toward the north and along Cardiac Hill into the main river right at Base Camp 1. The smaller stream ran perpendicular to the larger river and often was dry as a bone, but its mouth opened up right at the eastern part of the camp. Where the two bodies of water met, a pond had developed and created a great swimming hole about a hundred feet wide and fifty feet long before it flowed back down the granite and on to the west. The water was fairly warm due to the river and the small stream flowing miles upon miles over massive granite basins, which acted like solar panels heating the water before forming the pool. The pool at Base Camp 1 was about eight feet deep and a perfect place to go swimming if nobody was trying to fish. Yes, the pond contained mountain trout, which were hard to catch, but good to eat.

Around the pond stood a few trees. One spot in particular made for a perfect spot to set up a kitchen area. Water was easily accessible, and there was an area where we took huge pieces of granite to form chairs and even a table. It was below the main campsite and place where we would sit in the shade and relax, play cards, and eat our daily meals.

The main campsite itself had a flat dirt area about fifty feet away from the shore and about ten feet above the water's edge. The kitchen area was just below this and closer to the water's edge, but once you got away from the kitchen and the water, there were no trees to be found due to all the granite. The lack of trees actually made it a perfect place to set up tents, and have a campfire, plus there were hardly ever any mosquitos or pesky bugs to deal with during the day or at night. Since there were no bugs and no chances of rain most of the time, it was a perfect spot to lay outside and look at the stars. Most of the time it was so clear at night the Milky Way stood out as if it were a giant cloud of stars just floating by. Several times satellites could be seen with the naked eye as they made their way across the sky.

Base Camp 2

This campsite was also discovered by Mr. B, and it too was in a very remote location within the forest. It was about twelve miles east of Base Camp 1 and north of Yosemite National Park. It is approximately twenty miles (as the crow flies) from where we parked our cars, yet it seemed like a hundred when we were hiking to or from it. To get to this location we had to hike up hill for several miles from Base Camp 1 following the river, then at a particular location not shown on any map, we had to divert off the trail and basically follow our instinct and a forestry map to get to its location. There are no trails to this location, and only those who know where this camp is located will ever find it. It is located alongside a very remote river just north of Yosemite National Park, a river which flows past this base camp and then down a waterfall, which is approximately 200 feet tall. Most of the time we would do a day hike from Camp 3, and only a couple of times did we actually camp there. We never attempted to hike out from Base Camp 2 to our cars in one day, so we either hiked back to Base Camp 1, stay a night or two there, then hike out, or we would hike to Camp 3 and do the same thing. Either way it was a long way in, or a long way out, from where our cars were parked.

Camp 3

Exploring the miles and miles of pristine forests and mountain ranges north of Yosemite was what John and I liked to do. One trip we decided to explore more of the area and away from Base Camp 1 and 2. During this trip we decided to hike deeper into the forest and along a specific river where we found this amazing spot. This campsite was about eighteen to twenty miles from where we parked our cars, and it would typically take two days to get to it because of the terrain. Our first trip here started at Base Camp 1, and another trip, a couple of years later, lead us by a lake which was along a different trail that lead toward Camp 3. Either way, we would stop and camp a day or so before heading deeper into the Sierra Mountains to what we called Camp 3.

It was a long two-day hike to Camp 3, but once you got there it was amazing. The campsite sat near a beautiful mountain lake, which was surrounded by large granite mountains and a beautiful forest with loads of trees and foliage. The lake was approximately two miles long and a couple of hundred feet wide. The campsite sat out on a peninsula with a huge area to set up several tents and plenty of room to set up a nice campfire and kitchen area. There were signs of bear activity around the area, so we always hung our food in the trees and kept our camp extremely clean. We never had issues with bears, the only thing we saw were deer. The deer would walk through our camp almost every night and sometimes cause some concern when the larger deer came stomping through.

Camp 3 was and still is one of my favorite places to camp. It is an amazing location where it is easy to sit back and relax by the lakes edge, catch a fish or two, and have fun telling stories or maybe a practical joke or two.

End Note

For the thirty-five years I've been backpacking, there have been many other campsites John and I have taken people to, but these three are our main go-to locations and where we had fun playing our practical jokes on those who took the time and effort to go backpacking with us.

As with all our campsites, we would take extra time and care to make sure the camps were left the same way we found them, natural as possible and with limited to no signs a human had ever been there before. As a matter of fact, if someone were to hike to these locations they would probably swear nobody had ever set foot in them before.

Chapter 2

The Practical Joke That Started It All: "Oh No, It's Mr. Ranger"

My family would go camping every year when I was in grade school, and my dad taught my brothers and me the basics of camping in the woods such as how to pitch a tent, how to start a fire, how to fish, how to shoot, and even how to play a practical joke or two on your fellow campers. I felt comfortable in the woods, but I never put on a backpack or went off for a long hike until I was an adult. As an adult, backpacking was a new experience, although camping was not. I had camped several times in the woods and even had practical jokes played on me as a child while growing up. The practical jokes as a child were the basic rubber snake in the sleeping bag trick or the "let's go on a snipe hunt" gag. These were good, but not like the one Mr. B played on me in 1984.

As mentioned in the introduction of this book, it was the summer of 1983 when I went on my first backpacking trip with Mr. B. This trip consisted of Mr. B and three other guys who were about the same age as I, or a little younger. To my surprise, no practical jokes were played on me during this trip even though I was expecting them. This wasn't my first rodeo nor my first time camping, but it was the first time I ever carried a backpack and the first time I ever went backpacking with Mr. B who was known for his sense of humor. I expected something to be played on me, but nothing happened. Maybe that was the joke. Either way, backpacking was now in my blood and I had to go again and again.

When the trip was over, Mr. B said he probably wouldn't be going the following year and asked if I wanted to go. I wasn't sure, but I knew if I did go I would have to plan the trip on my own. I was talking to a coworker and friend of mine, John, about the trip I had just gotten home from and how much I enjoyed it. He said he would be interested if I planned a trip for next year. So in the spring of 1984 I called Frank, one of the guys who went with me the previous year, and asked him if he would like to join John and me on a seven-day backpacking trip to the same area where Mr. B took us. He said yes, and the trip was on. In order to make sure I knew what I was doing, I went to Mr. B and got more information about the area, where to get permits, and any helpful hints he could give me. I made sure to tell him the dates I planned on going, the locations I planned on camping, and the dates I planned on moving from one area to another.

The following is the practical joke that started it all. It was a joke that was played on me and one I will never forget. I laugh about it every time I tell it. I call it "Hey, Mr. Ranger."

The Setup

It all started in June 1984, when Mr. B called me about a month prior to John, Frank, and I heading out on our adventure. Mr. B said he heard forest rangers were doing several spot checks on backpacker in the back country. He said they were looking for permits, checking campsites to see if the campers were following their guidelines, making sure the backpackers had fire permits, and things of this nature. He said to make sure to get the various permits and be prepared for a forest ranger to visit our campsite. I thought this was a bit crazy since the Base Camp 1 and the other locations were miles off the beaten path and no trails even came close to the area, but Mr. B had connections and I felt his advice was legitimate. So of course I made sure I did everything Mr. B suggested.

A few days prior to us heading to the mountains, Mr. B called again and asked if I could confirm the date I planned on getting back home and to go over the trip one more time. He wanted to confirm the area where we planned on camping along with the dates we planned on being at each spot. He said he had misplaced this information I gave him a few months prior and thought it would be a good idea to review it and mark it down on one of his maps just in case I didn't return home on schedule. This made sense since he knew we had two locations where we were planning on hiking, one was about eighteen miles from where we parked our car and the other was another fifteen miles or more past that. It was my thought that if we encountered a problem or suffered an injury that kept us from hiking out and getting back home on the date I told him, he would be able to tell the rescue team, based on dates and the map, exactly where we were. So of course I gave him this information. I didn't give this a second thought since Mr. B knew the area like the back of his hand. Plus, I had given this information to my wife already, so why not give a copy of it to Mr. B?

The Joke: "Hey, Mr. Ranger"
Location: Base Camp 1

After driving for twelve hours, John and I met up with my other friend, Frank, at his family cabin prior to hiking in the next morning. That afternoon we went to a local market where we bumped into a friend of Frank by the name of Sam. Sam and Frank had hiked with Mr. B several years before and knew each other really well. While we were talking to Sam, Frank asked me if Sam could join us on the hike. I said, "Sure, the more the better." So Frank asked Sam if he could join us, but he said he had to work and couldn't make the trip. So the next morning John, Frank, and I hiked to Base Camp 1 where we thought it would be just the three of us.

We had been at Base Camp 1 for two days and were planning on taking a day hike on day 3 up to a lake north of us. So on the third morning we packed a day-pack and headed up to the lake. This lake was about three miles away and up a huge granite mountain. We had to hike up Cardiac Hill, along the small stream that flowed from the north to a meadow about three miles away. Once at the meadow we had to turn to the east and hike up another very steep granite face to the lake we wanted to swim and hike around. This day hike took us almost all day. We returned back to camp around four in the afternoon.

That night, after we ate dinner and cleaned up, we sat down by the campfire talking about the day. It was around eight in the evening when it started to get dark and the fire's glow was the only light we had. The moon wasn't out and the stars were starting to fill the sky. John was sitting to my right looking up toward the north and the mountains beyond that which we had climbed earlier that day. I was looking to the east, and Frank was sitting to my left looking at the stars. We were talking about how strange it would be to see some old man, with a hundred-year-old beard, running down the granite with a bear chasing him or some crazy mountain man just walking into camp. We were all making up dumb stories and telling jokes when all of a sudden John looked up toward the north and said, "Hey, there's a couple of flashlights heading our way." I didn't believe him since we were miles off the beaten path, and who in their right mind would hike down a steep mountain like Cardiac Hill to get to where we were located? But sure enough, there were two flashlights heading our way.

We thought it might be a couple of lost hikers, so we waited for their arrival. It took about ten minutes before the two flashlights arrived in our camp. The flashlights belonged to two young forest rangers. They said they were in our camp earlier that day and they were inspecting campsites in the area. They said their inspections were based on the rules and regulations listed within our permit. They asked for our permits and stood there for a minute or two. We said we were out on a day hike and that's why we weren't in camp when they came by earlier. They didn't seem to care and only said that when they were in our camp they noticed we were not far enough away from the water's edge and we had to move our camp because we broke the rules in the permit. They said they wouldn't fine us if we moved it and didn't give them any static.

It was about eight forty-five in the evening, very dark, and we were very tired from our day hike. None of us wanted to start tearing down our camp. So we did what every good backpacker would do, we tried to reason with these two rangers, but they wouldn't budge. I even tried to play my wildcard by saying I was a firefighter and I understand the rules, but couldn't it wait until morning. The two rangers said they would let us wait until morning, but they were new rangers and their supervisors were checking up on them. So since their supervisors would be pissed off if we weren't complying, they had no say in the matter. Apparently the rangers had issues with a few other campers at a lake to the northeast of us and the supervisors ended up fining them for not complying with their demands. So the two rangers in our camp advised us that we better comply or risk getting fined. They said if we weren't tearing down our camp by the time their supervisors, who were heading down the mountain, got there, we would be fined. I looked up toward the north, and sure enough two more flashlights were heading our way.

We tried and tried to reason with the first two rangers, but they stuck their ground and ordered us to tear down our camp. They even told us we had to move our tent, which I knew was properly set up in an area that met the guidelines of the permits; there was no reason to tear down our tent, so I waited until the supervisors got to camp to discuss this further. However, John and I, along with Frank, started to move our kitchen, tear down the rock chairs we had made and the rock table we took hours to put into place. We were moving everything we could before the supervisors walked into camp.

Soon the two other flashlights, the supervisors, were in our camp. They perched themselves above the camp looking down on us from a higher viewpoint shining their flashlights here and there. One of them decided to move toward us to make sure we were tearing down the kitchen and moving our stuff. As he walked toward the kitchen area, Frank noticed something about him. This ranger had a particular gait to his walk, a gait that Sam, Frank's friend, had. Frank said to me he knew only one guy who walked like that, and it was Sam, the guy we asked to go backpacking with us a few days ago. So we approached him and said, "Hey, you look like a friend of ours, what's your name?" He quickly said, "Bob," and that's when it hit us, this wasn't a ranger and his name wasn't Bob, it was Sam! This ranger, "Bob," however didn't have long bushy sideburns like our friend Sam had a few days ago, so we asked him again what his name was. Basically we weren't 100 percent sure if this guy was really Bob, or Frank's friend, Sam. While we were trying to make him confess his name wasn't "Bob" the other supervisor decided to say something. He said, in a very clear and determined voice, "This place looks like a shit hole." As soon as he spoke those words, I knew in an instant who this voice belonged to. It was Mr. B in the flesh.

Frank had hiked with Mr. B in the past, he and I both knew it was Mr. B and we started to laugh our butts off. Unfortunately John had never met Mr. B, so he thought Frank and I were going crazy and kept on destroying our camp. Frank was laughing so hard that he fell to the ground laughing and saying we just got pranked. I had to stop John from tearing down the rest of our camp and tell him we were set up and the joke was on us.

Mr. B planned this entire joke months prior to our ever leaving. He contacted Sam, a.k.a. "Bob," who lived near the town we would hike out of, and asked him if he would like to play a practical joke on me and my two friends. He didn't hesitate, and that is why he turned us down when we asked if he would like to join us on the backpacking trip. Mr. B also asked Sam to get two other guys to help out with the gag.

Mr. B knew exactly where I would be, when I would be moving to the next camp, and what day I would be taking my friends on a day hike, he had it all set. He would play out his practical joke the day we went on our day hike. So Mr. B drove twelve hours from Arizona to the small town in the Sierra Nevada Mountains north of Yosemite, hooked up with his co-practical jokers, packed fake uniforms, fake mustaches, food for one day, and prepared his band of jokesters with the setup. The day he knew we would go on our day hike was the day he got these guys to hike well over sixteen miles to a spot near the meadow above our camp and camp there until it started to get dark. He wrote out a script and gave it to one of the young guys who joined him. He told him to say he was a new ranger and that he and his supervisors were inspecting campsites. From there Mr. B told him to just read the script and do not deviate from it. He knew I'd try to talk my way out of tearing down my camp, so he told the kid, "Just keep on reading the script and use a pencil to check off the lines as you read them." This kid was only fourteen years old by the way, and he got me good. Not only did he wear a fake uniform, he wore a fake mustache and spoke in a deep voice. He played his part extremely well. As for Sam, he actually shaved off his bushy side burns the night before he hiked in with Mr. B just to make sure we wouldn't recognize him.

That night and the next morning we laughed for hours about how we literally destroyed our camp all based on a young fourteen-year-old kid reading a script and telling us his supervisors made him do it. We couldn't believe the amount of effort Mr. B had to put toward this joke. Who in their right mind would drive twelve hours, hike another eight, and wait in the dark to hike down a mountain like Cardiac Hill to pull a gag like this? Then, the next morning pack up their stuff and hike all the way out and drive another twelve hours back to Arizona. It was crazy! While Mr. B and his practical jokers headed back to his car sixteen miles away, John and I, along with Frank, headed to Base Camp 2 wondering if more rangers would be stopping by.

From this trip forward, when camping at Base Camp 1, John and I would find ourselves telling the story of how Mr. B played the best practical joke ever on us and how we fell for it hook, line, and sinker. We almost always had to tell the "Hey, Mr. Ranger" story at Base Camp 1 because it was easier to point out where everything was and we didn't have to explain to how difficult it was to get to this campsite. This alone made it easier to explain the effort Mr. B and his fellow jokesters had to go through to pull of such a joke. It was amazing!

The next time you're in the woods and you see flashlights coming toward your camp, make sure you check their ID, pull on their mustaches, and check their clipboards for a possible handwritten script before you start to destroy your campsite. It could be Mr. B and his team of jokesters paying you a visit.

Chapter 3

How Old Is That Poop?

This is a practical joke I have played on several people, on a variety of backpacking and hiking trips, and especially on those who have never experienced the great outdoors. When my daughters were younger they asked me to play this joke on their Girl Scout troop when I took them on a hike in the desert near our home in Arizona. Using smaller animals as a reference, the joke works particularly well while hiking along a trail or even near camp. The animal that is referenced should be smaller in size, but with this joke, size does matter. I recommend referencing the fake poop to a deer, a muskrat, or even a squirrel while playing this joke on one person or a group of people. I'd stay away from discussing bear scat or larger animals. This joke wouldn't work with that size of droppings.

The joke works almost every time, and it's a lot of fun to see the reactions of those watching you examine the dark little morsels while pulling off the joke. I love to see the facial expressions of the people who are unaware of the fact I'm joking with them. I particularly like to watch their eyes bug out while I'm doing my part to act like a knowledgeable hunter or a wildlife expert. It's very hard to keep a straight face when doing this, but it's a must if you want to pull off this joke.

Have fun with this one, but make sure not to accidentally use the real stuff, it wouldn't be healthy and it would be really disgusting.

The Setup

A few days prior to going on a hike or backpacking trip, I would prepare the gag. There are two items I have used to pull off this gag, feel free to use either one, but not both. I personally found item #1 to work the best for me. But feel free to be creative.

1) I would buy some trail mix and pull out the pieces of rolled-up, dried dates. The dried dates tend to look like dried pieces of muskrat, rabbit, or squirrel poop, but with a little effort you can make them look like deer poop. This stuff works great because it has small particles of other items in it, which helps with the joke; or

2) Feel free to buy some small "tootsie rolls." Then break off small portions of them, roll them up into oblong balls so they resemble deer droppings. Not that I know a lot about deer droppings, but I've seen a few piles of it in my day and they are about a half inch long and one-fourth inch round.

Note: Tootsie roll deer droppings tend to stick together, so don't pack them deep in the bottom of the backpack, it's not easy to break them apart once they've stuck together. Plus, don't squeeze other items around them, this turns everything into one big blob.

Whatever product selected to make the fake poop, make sure there is a good handful of either item so the initial pile looks real and as large as a person would expect.

Place the fake droppings in a Ziploc plastic bag and then place them somewhere in the backpack or day-pack so it can be easily accessible while hiking down the trail or while camping in the woods. Try not to squish the little darlings together, they need to look as fresh as possible and easily picked up or pulled apart when playing the joke on some unsuspecting soul.

The Joke: How Old Is That Poop?
Location: On the trail or somewhere near camp

John and I had a friend of ours from work join us one year on a backpacking trip. He had been on a trip with us before and this time he asked if he could bring his two boys with him; his boys were in their early teenage years. I said sure, and my mind started to think of what kind of a joke I could play on them. Then it hit me, these guys would be perfect for the ole' "how old is that poop?" gag.

This backpacking trip was a nine-day trip. We spent some time at Base Camp 1, but due to the terrain the gag wouldn't work until we were actually where we could see some deer or maybe some musk-rats now and then. So I waited until we hiked to Camp 3 where the trees were denser and the lake provided a great place for deer to hang out as well as the nearby rocks for muskrats. One day as we were going on a day hike near Camp 3, I decided to play this practical joke on my friend's two sons. My friend knew all about the joke and said it would be fun to see what his boys would do.

While we were hiking along, I was pointing out interesting facts about the plants, animals, and other things in the area. I told the boys to keep an eye out for deer and other smaller game animals like musk-rats and squirrels because I wanted to show them a trick I learned from a friend who was a very experienced hunter. I told the boys the hunter had all kind of tricks to track animals and how to tell where and when the last time the animals were in the area. So the hunt was on for animals and their poop. As we were hiking along, I'd contin-ued to point out things that made it look like I was some kind of wilderness expert and knew what I was talking about. Little did they know, I don't know much about hunting, or tracking, let alone what kind of plants we were looking at. I just made it up as we went along. Soon I found an opportunity to run down the trail a bit to set up the gag. I ran about a hundred feet, dropped the fake poop droppings in a very conspicuous location, then turned around and ran back to wait for the guys to catch up. I quickly found a rocky area to sit on that had a few critters running around. As they approached I acted as if I had been sitting there awhile waiting for them to catch up.

Once they got to me I asked if they saw the muskrat that was on the rocky area we had just passed by. They said they hadn't, so I said maybe we can figure out how often this muskrat or possibly deer were last in this area. I said to the boys, "Start looking for their scat, or deer dropping," which they took on as if it were a challenge to see who could find poop the fastest. I told them it shouldn't be too difficult to find if we think like a muskrat or deer. It sounded corny to me when I told them to think like a deer or muskrat, but they bought it and took on the challenge.

At first I thought the boys might think it strange that we should be looking for poop in the forest, but that's what we started to do. As we approached the fake pile of poop, I made sure the boys found it first. Their eyes lit up with excitement when they found the pile of what they thought was the real deal. Almost simultaneously they said, "Hey, I think we found a pile of poop," which made me laugh on the inside, but I had to show the "hunter" within me and act real serious. I proceeded to the pile with an attitude of confidence that I would show these boys how a real hunter tracks and stalks their prey. Once I got to the boys and the pile of fake poop, I said, "Yup, that looks like muskrat poop all right, now let me show you how to determine how long it's been since these critters laid this pile down." I proceeded to pick up a stick and start poking at the pile of fake poop. As I poked at it, I told them you can tell by the way the poop laid on the ground which direction the animal was heading. After I told them that, I slowly reached toward the pile and picked up a small handful of the fake poop, about four or five pieces. When I picked up the poop and placed it within my hands, the boys made a few comments like, "that's sick" or "dude, that is gross." I even looked at them when I did this, and their facial expressions verified it more that they thought I was gross especially when they both winced their eyes a little.

Once I had the small morsels of fake poop in my hands, I took one piece and squished it between my fingers exposing the inside of the fake poop. The boys got a little more grossed out by this and even said, "Dude, what are you doing?" I said, "This is how you can tell what the animal was eating and this helps identify if they were grazing in the area or not." As I spread the fake poop in my fingers, I started to point at the smaller objects within the fake poop while saying, "Here, you can see what this critter was eating prior to pooping." I pointed at small bushes and shrubs in the area keeping a straight face and continuing to say, "Look at this poop, see what this guy has been eating, they must have been eating this plant and that one over there," as I pointed at a variety of plants nearby.

After I showed them what was inside the fake poop, I brought the squished morsels closer and closer to my nose. I then told them the smell will help determine if it's a male or a female. I smelt it for a short period of time as if I was trying to smell every part of its inner and outer layers. Soon I could see it in the boys' faces that they couldn't believe I was really doing this, smelling poop found lying on the ground. (The five-second rule does not apply here.) As I looked at the boys, I could see it in their facial expressions that they thought I was some crazy mountain man.

Now that I really had their attention, it was time to seal the deal. It was time to reach back down to the pile of fake poop and grab a fairly large handful of the stuff. Once I grabbed up a good handful, I shook it in my hand as if I was getting ready to roll a pair of dice. I hesitated for effect and then tossed the fairly large handful of fake poop into my mouth, chewed on it with a disgusting look upon my face (as if this fake poop was the real deal), and quickly spit it out. Once I spit it out, I grabbed a quick drink of water from my canteen and said, "This poop is about two weeks old." At this point the boys were about to puke.

After the boys were done making their own puking sounds, I decided to give them the opportunity to see if they would be interested in trying a bite, but they looked at me as if I bumped my head or maybe they thought the poop was making me delirious. Either way, their dad, who knew all about this gag, stepped up to the dinner table and decided to play along with me. Their dad said he saw me do this before and back then he turned me down, but this time he was going to try tasting it. So he reached down and took one small piece of the fake poop and slowly took a very small nibble of it to prove to his boys he was a man too. Once he tasted it, he told his boys that the taste wasn't as bad as he thought it would be. After that, their dad convinced the boys to try a bite. To my surprise they actually picked up a piece and took a very, very small nibble of one piece. They quickly spit it out and said that was gross, and off down the trail we went. The rest of the trip they stayed clear of any poop.

About a week after the backpacking trip, I had everyone over to my house for a BBQ. During the BBQ. we shared stories and photos of our adventure. Soon one of the boys started to tell the story of how I ate some muskrat poop and how I picked at it, squished it in my fingers, smelled it, and then took a handful of it and tossed it in my mouth. What they didn't know was everyone else at the BBQ was in on the gag and said they knew I did it all the time. Soon I left the room and brought back a bowl full of the dried dates that looked like the poop the boys saw me eat on the backpacking trip. I offered it to everyone to try; to the boys' surprise everyone joined in on eating the fake poop. It was at this point the boys realized they were set up and the poop they saw me eat was just a joke. Everyone laughed, and the boys had fun retelling their side of the story again and again.

So the next time you're out in the woods and you come across a pile of what looks like some kind of animal poop, think twice before you eat it. It could be the real deal or it could be someone playing a practical joke on you.

Chapter 4

The Amazing Fire Rock

This "Fire Rock" joke was originated and conducted by my friend Frank on his backpacking buddies, who then passed the joke on to me to use on my friends and fellow hikers. This joke takes a little bit of salesmanship to convince those going on the trip that it's the real deal—an amazing "Fire Rock."

When I heard about the gag I thought I'd modify it a bit and try it out on some of my friends. Frank told me how he did the joke and that he would wrap a large rock in aluminum foil and then tell his backpacking friends it was a "Fire Rock" he used on his last expedition into the woods. The rock he used was one he got from his backyard and it weighed about ten pounds. He also said he put it into a fire pit to make sure it had ashes and soot on it to make it look like a used, burnt stone. He called it a "Fire Rock," and so did I.

I took the joke to a different level as you will soon see. To this day I never thought I could find someone who would be so gullible to really believe the story and purposely place a ten-pound rock into the depths of their backpack, but sure enough, there are people out there who will believe almost anything

This joke is meant to be played on the person who says his backpack never weighs that much. Boy, can you change that in a jiffy.

The Setup

Prior to going on the backpacking trip, a flyer such as the one shown below needs to be made. This flyer will then be wrapped around an everyday, fairly large, dark-colored rock and then secured in place with some clear cellophane. The flyer that I created looks like this:

At the end of this chapter is a more detailed view of this flyer. The flyer has information on how to use the "Fire Rock," and for an added bonus there is a fake barcode at the bottom right corner along with the price it might cost for such a stone in either the USA or in Canada. That is of course if someone actually desires to have one of his friends believe the rock was purchased at a local sporting goods store and would carry this hunk of rock on his next backpacking trip.

The rock shouldn't weigh over ten pounds. A five- or six-pound rock is best. The size of the rock should be about eight inches long and anywhere from three to four inches round if possible. A dark-colored rock works best for the gag since it adds more to the sales pitch when setting up the person who is willing to carry it. Once a rock has been selected, wrap the flyer around the rock and then use some quality plastic wrap or cellophane to seal up the package so it looks like something that was bought at a sporting goods store. Make sure to make the edges of the cellophane as clean and neat of a seal as possible. If it looks sloppy the joke won't work. To make the gag work even better, get a bag from a sporting goods store to place the rock in. This gives the effect that it was purchased along with other items from a real store. (Funny what a plastic bag from a sporting goods store can do for setting up this story.)

Now that the rock, wrapped in the flyer and covered in the cellophane, has been constructed, place it in the sporting goods bag and get ready to carry out the joke.

The way this joke works best is to tell all the guys who are going on the backpacking or camping trip with you to meet at your house about a day or two before the trip. The reason for this meeting is to go over all the details about the trip one more time, to answer any questions the guys may have, and to hand out the food and group supplies you have gathered for the trip. I personally have taken guys on backpacking trips who have never camped, let alone hiked, for miles into the woods. Since many of the guys who have gone backpacking with John and me have had limited to no experience backpacking, the meeting actually did make them feel more at ease, and it allowed me to set the joke into motion a lot easier. Usually my friend John and I would organize the entire trip and purchase all the supplies and divide up any community items based on how many guys were going with us. So during the group meeting, I knew I had to have someone in on the joke to make the gag work. John had since moved away, so I had to pick another friend of mine to help me out. They were the one who set the ball in motion. Note: If there isn't someone you trust in pulling off the gag, the initial setup will be a lot harder to sell. Not everyone is gullible when it comes to carrying a large rock in his backpack.

The Joke: The Amazing "Fire Rock"
Location: The joke starts out at home and ends whenever the
timing is right. Typically the gag ends while on the trail or at your
first campsite.

About two or three days prior to heading out for the backpacking trip, a meeting should be called requiring everyone to stop by and discuss the trip one more time and to pick up additional supplies which were purchased for the group. Spouses or significant others are always welcome to join in on these meetings since they too should know where everyone is heading and when they all should be back home safe and sound.

When everyone is gathered for the meeting, I would start the conversation by reviewing the dates, location, and important things everyone should bring in their backpacks. I'd then start handing out group items to the guys. The group items were things I had purchased that everyone would use at one point or another during the trip. Each of the guys would be handed a bag with items, which were divided up based on weight. This was a normal practice, and by the time the bags were almost all handed out, I'd ask what everyone else was bringing on the trip and how heavy their backpacks were. Then I'd wait for the one person to say how light his backpack was and how much room he had. This was the guy I would be looking for to set the trap. Once my partner in crime and I knew who had the lightest backpack, my partner in crime would ask the all-important question: "Who is carrying the "Fire Rock?" This very important question must be asked with a straight face and with a tone in the voice that is of regret for even asking such a dumb question. The question should bring a few strange looks from the group, but stay calm and start to fumble around looking for the sporting goods bag with the "Fire Rock" in it. Once the bag is in hand, look at the guy who bragged about his backpack being the lightest in the group. This is the guy who is the one you want to carry the rock, if not, pick the next gullible person, either way, you need to pick someone. What also works is that while the "Fire Rock" is being pulled out, I would say I carried it last year and I'm not carrying it again and the person who is in on the joke would say he carried it the year before that. This leaves the door open for someone else to volunteer to carry the Fire Rock.

Now is the time to open the bag and pull out the "Fire Rock," which is neatly wrapped up in the cellophane. The facts about the rock need to be explained to the group. I found it best to tell the group a friend of mine turned me on to this rock and it has never failed me yet. I'd tell them the following story to sell the joke. Being a good story teller, okay, a good liar, works best at selling the story. If a straight face cannot be maintained while telling the story, the joke won't work. What's fun about this gag is if the group figures out the fire rock is just a joke, everyone will still get a great laugh about it. As for the sales pitch, it goes like this:

> I purchase a rock like this every time I go camping, whether it's been camping with my family in a campground or out in the woods on my backpacking trip, I always bring one of these rocks with me. I'm not sure what the properties of this rock are, or if they added an additive to it, but it has always worked for me. One time it rained for three days straight, but once I got the rock out and made sure it was dry, soon after hitting it with my knife I had a fire within minutes and I never lost the flame once. It's amazing how it works. The only thing I hate about it is that it weighs a bit much, but it's well worth the weight when it starts to rain or when you can't keep a flame going. Now the question is, who wants to carry it?

At this point I would always hope the macho guy in the group would step up to the plate and volunteer, but it didn't always turn out that way, so I had to pick a person and run with it. Next, try to read the flyer the rock is wrapped in without opening it. Tell the group the following:

I don't want to open the package of the rock. It tends to smell sometimes, and I hate to have that smell in my backpack. Plus, I don't know if the rock would ignite something in my backpack if it rubbed up on something. So whoever is going to carry it, I highly suggest it is wrapped in a separate cloth or something.

Everyone will want to open it and smell the rock, but don't let this happen. Soon the rock will be passed around the group as if everyone is trying to believe such a thing exists. They will all want to read the flyer the rock is wrapped in, and some may even want to see how it works before the trip. Whatever it takes, keep the rock in its wrapper.

Once a volunteer has stepped up to the plate or someone had to be picked, I had to decide how long I wanted to play out the joke. I suggest one of the following, with the third option being the best:

1) I would tell them the rock is a joke at the trailhead prior to setting one foot into the woods. This would typically cause the rock to be pulled out, the wrapper to be ripped off, and the rock to be tossed in the woods. The flyer of course would be kept for prosperity sake, and we would laugh about the gag while hiking along the trail.

Note: There is a health risk involved with the following two options and this joke. If the person is told about the fake "Fire Rock" while on the trail or when they've hiked for miles and miles to get to camp, I suggest standing far away from the person who is about to be told the "Fire Rock" is joke. The person carrying the rock *will* want to put the "Fire Rock" in a place where the sun doesn't shine, and I don't mean under your tent or in your sleeping bag. One thing for sure, he won't be happy he was made to carry a ten-pound rock for no reason. Make sure to remind him he volunteered to carry it. Also, he will not be very happy he actually believed there is such a thing as an amazing "Fire Rock."

2) Sometimes I'd wait until I've been on the trail for a few miles or when I see the person carrying the rock is more tired than the rest of the group. This is when I know the rock should be removed so the guy won't pass out.

3) Lastly, I'd wait to tell them the rock is a joke once we got to camp, and typically when it was time to start a fire. That is when the "Fire Rock" is opened from its wrapper and we try to use it like the package says, but it doesn't work.

Here are some other adlibs which can be tossed out to set the hook deeper!

- I'd say I had issues with the first "Fire Rock" I purchased, but after contacting the company they told me how to best set the rock into a fire pit by setting it in a specific way, standing upright and toward the center of the pit. Once I found this out, it worked every time.

- The reason why the rock is so dark is that it acts like a solar panel where it contracts and stores the heat from the fire and the sun. This feature helps the Fire Rock to reignite easier the next time it is used.

- The weight of the rock is due to the properties of the rock and the additives the company soaks the rock in prior to packaging it for sale.

- I found out the rocks are mined in Virginia near some coal mine, which explains how the Fire Rock works.

- I like to use my knife to create a spark, breaking it in half doesn't work that well and it causes a mess once the Fire Rock is split.

- Each time I've used a Fire Rock it tends to reduce in size and I found the Fire Rock is good for starting about four to five fires. Trips over seven or eight days required me to pack two Fire Rocks, but the weather looks good for this trip and we only need to pack one.

- Last but not least, I would say I read it on the Internet where "everything is true."

Whatever made-up facts that can be added to the story to make it more believable, the better the chances someone will believe it and the better chances the "Fire Rock" will join you on your next back-packing adventure.

Remember to stand behind something when the joke has been unveiled. The person who carried the rock or believed in the story may have a good arm and might toss the rock in your direction.

"Fire Rock"

The Only Fire Starter Any Backpacker Will Ever Need

The amazing "Fire Rock" starts fire with only a spark from a knife or by breaking the rock in two pieces and utilizing friction to start the initial blaze. Once the "Fire Rock" has started your fire, remove this rock from the flames and sit it nearby so it can be heated by the fire you just created.

The "Fire Rock" can be wrapped in aluminum foil to retain its heat and be used again to start your next fire or to warm your sleeping bag or clothes if desired. Once the "Fire Rock" has been heated, it can be carried safely in your backpack to your next campsite within a 12 hour period and used to start your next fire by only placing small pieces of kindling upon it. Within minutes a flame will occur and your "Fire Rock" can be removed from the flame and saved for your next campsite. If rain or inclement weather is expected, cover your "Fire Rock" in a dry, but cool area so moisture will not cause the rock to lose its warming properties.

Do Not store this "Fire Rock" near any combustible materials or a heat source due to its incendiary properties unless it is cool to the touch.

Remember "Only you can prevent Fires, so please handle responsibly.

For questions or to report a problem, please contact our customer service department at: www.firerock.com

0 36000 29145 2

$ 8.99 U.S.
$ 17.50 Can

Chapter 5

Gold Miners Exploding Dirt

Earlier in this book I wrote about the two boys who watched me eat fake poop, thinking I was eating the real deal. Well, it seems my friend with his two boys liked backpacking so much that a year or two after I played the fake poop trick on them, the boys and their father wanted to join John and me on one more adventure into the woods. However, this time the boys were keen to my practical jokes and were keeping an eye on me. What's great about this trip was they weren't aware that my backpacking buddy, John, was a really good storyteller too and we had a joke all ready to be played one more time on the unsuspecting duo. John and I had played this joke on others in previous years, and this time we knew the boys didn't trust us and we had to lead up to the joke days in advance so not to look too suspicious.

This trip included about six people, two of whom were the teenage boys and the rest were some good friends who knew all about John and my practical joking. They were jokesters too, so don't think we were the only two in the group to keep an eye out for foul play. Besides, this year was John's turn to set the stage and to reel the boys in for a joke we called the "Exploding Dirt" trick.

The Setup

The setup for this joke is fairly easy; when I go backpacking I usually bring a box or two of pancake mix which only requires water to make the batter. I've used other product which had a flour base in it, but I found pancake mix works best. When nobody is looking, take some pancake mix, or anything with flour, and pour a couple of piles of the powder under a couple of rocks around the campsite. When deciding where to hide the powder it's best to place the powder in an area where it will be easy to find later, especially when it's dark. Also, depending on the story that needs to be made up to sell the joke, think about how the powder would get in such a spot in the first place. This is important when telling the story and getting the people to believe what is being told and, more importantly, why it may or may not be found in other areas around camp.

The Joke: Exploding Dirt
Location: Around the campfire when it's nice and dark

When my friend John and I played this trick, we knew we would be camping at Base Camp 1 for a few days, so John thought it would be a good idea to bring a plastic miner's pan with him to help sell the story. This way we could take a couple of days to set up the boys for the exploding dirt trick. The year we played this trick on the boys was when the weather was just amazing. We would swim, fish, and play in the swimming hole near our camp most of the day, then at night we would sit by the campfire telling stories and checking out the stars above. A couple of days while at Base Camp 1 John got out his miner's pan and went off panning for gold along the river, at least that's what he told the boys who sometimes would follow him.

One night, while we were sitting around the campfire telling stories, I asked John if he found anything in the river with his miner's pan. He said he didn't, but he thought there were other minerals in the river and around our base camp that were interesting. This peaked the boys' interests. John started to set the trap by saying he found particles, or a powdery substance, in the soil that was typical of the powder he read about in a book on mining. He said the book discussed how miners in remote areas found a powdery substance similar to what he thought he found earlier in the day, but powder mentioned in the book was not as powerful as gunpowder. He said the book mentioned how the miners couldn't haul in gun powder and other heavy supplies deep into the forests while looking for gold, so they would use this powdery substance they discovered to help blast small rocks apart. The book went on to say the powdery substance wasn't that powerful, but it would cause a flash strong enough to break apart small rocks. John went on to say that based on all the granite in the area, and the fact the water would flow through our camp when it rained or during the spring runoff, the granite helped grind the minerals out of the rock. John said he thought he found some small pockets of this powder right near our camp.

At this point, the boys were listening but not paying close attention to John's story, but that was soon to change. As the campfire was burning, the rest of the group and I were sitting around talking about the next days' hike to a nearby lake. Nobody was really paying too much attention to John, but he was still involved with the practical joke, which was about to get real. As the others were talking, John was pretending to chip away at the nearby granite with another rock. He acted as if he was gathering some of its dust particles, then without making a production about it, he stood up, walked to the fire, and threw the dust he gathered into the fire. As the dust hit the fire it flashed, everyone took notice. Of course anytime you toss flour or pancake mix into a fire it will flash. Do not try this at home!

John had officially set the hook, and the boys were about to be played. As soon as the fire flashed, the boys jumped up and asked, "What was that?" John said he had chipped away some of the granite rock to see if it had the substance he had read about, and sure enough it did. Well, at least the boys thought it did. The two boys quickly went into their tent, grabbed their metal spoons and forks, and started to chip away at the rocks. John also continued to chip away at the rock to create more dust. Soon John would toss in another handful of the powdery substance and the fire would flash once again. Remember, this is only a small handful of pancake mix.

As the boys gathered up a couple of small handfuls of dust and dirt in their hands, they ran to the campfire and tossed their dust at the fire. However, the boys' dust and dirt didn't contain any pancake mix, so it didn't flash, it did however almost put out the fire. They asked John why their dust didn't work, and he said they were probably digging in the wrong area. He then pointed them to a different area as we all sat and watched to see what the boys would do next. After a few minutes, John would gather some more of his "pancake" dust, casually stand up, walk to the fire, and toss it in for another flash to transpire. The boys would try too, but to no avail.

John, knowing the boys would start to question why their handfuls of dirt didn't work, decided to get up and help the boys gather some dust, which of course contained pancake mix. The "pancake" dust and dirt John helped the boys gather of course allowed them to experience some "exploding dirt" in their hands. This way the boys would not lose hope and would continue to mine this amazing substance. Once the boys were able to toss dirt into the fire and cause it to flash, they went right back to work chipping away at the granite as if they were digging to China. Time and time again they would toss their particles into the fire, and time and time again nothing would happen unless John helped them out. The boys figured that John must be the expert, so they asked him for more help, and soon the three of them were scraping up piles of dust, sometimes it worked and sometimes it wouldn't. The only time it worked of course is was when John handed them some of the dust he collected with the pancake mix added. (You would think these boys would have figured it out, but nope, they kept on chipping away at the rock.)

After about an hour of the boys chipping away at the rocks and not being able to make the fire flash unless John helped, the sound of their spoons and forks striking the granite started to get annoying. The boys' father asked them to stop chipping away at the stone and said they were destroying their eating utensils. The boys quickly pointed out that the fork and spoon they were using wasn't theirs, but were their father's. Hearing this, everyone around the campfire started laughing their butts off, except their dad of course.

The boys ended up putting away their dad's beaten up and bent utensils, but John decided to show them an easier way to collect the powdery substance. He reached under a specific rock, grabbed some dust that was lying there in a neat little pile, and then used it to cause the fire to flash. This went on until all the powder was gone. Soon the powdery substance was all gone and the boys couldn't do their magic anymore. This was when John got to explain to the boys that he had another box of exploding dirt in the kitchen area and the dirt was not as real as they thought. He showed the boys a box of pancake mix and said, "It's amazing how pancake mix can flash once it's tossed into the fire, I wonder how it got under this rock in the first place?" At this point the boys knew they were pranked. They just sat there and laughed at themselves and at their dad because they destroyed his eating utensils for no reason at all.

The next time pancakes are served on a camping trip, watch out for the story of exploding dirt to be mentioned when the fire is bright and someone in the group is known for practical jokes. Once the story is told, and the mining begins, be careful to protect the eating utensils, they may become digging tools, especially if there are teenage boys who want to dig up more of the mysterious powder for themselves.

Chapter 6

Can We Have Your Initials Please?

For almost twenty years John and I would camp at Base Camp 1, and each time we would typically bring someone new along to experience this amazing area. Almost every time we camped at Base Camp 1 we would plan a day hike to a very beautiful mountain lake about three hours away. In order to get to this lake we would hike up the granite mountain to the north of Base Camp 1, turn left at a specific meadow, and then head up a steep granite mountain face, some would call it a cliff, but we just knew it to be very steep. It rose several hundreds of feet above the meadow, and once at the top we would have to hike another mile or so before we got to the lake. The hike was a bit tough, but once we got to the lake we would forget about the hike and focus more on the lake's beauty and the fact it was time to take a cool and refreshing dip. Unless of course we played a practical joke on one of our friends.

On this one adventure it was only John and me, and my friend Gary, who headed out into the woods. We had planned on meeting Mr. B at Base Camp 1 and knew he was already there a day ahead of us, so we planned on camping with him and his two friends prior to the three of us hiking deeper into the mountains. Once at Base Camp 1 we did the usual things, but this time Mr. B was there to help me set up another practical joke: the joke we later called "Can we have your initials please?"

The Setup

The joke should be played on someone new to the group. It won't work on someone who has hiked with the group in the past and, more importantly, one who has hiked to various locations on past adventures. Next there is, of course, the story that needs to be created for this joke to work. Making the story more of a tradition works best to convince the new camper that the story about to be unveiled is a tradition everyone in the past has honored. It is then up to this newbie, with a little pressure and convincing from those who know it's a joke, which he too will participate in the tradition.

The Joke: Can We Have Your Initials Please?
Location: The joke starts at camp and should be "carried" out miles away at a specific destination picked in advance.

John and I, along with my friend Gary, had been in Base Camp 1 for a couple of days with Mr. B and his group. During the first day or two, I had the chance to talk to Mr. B in private about playing a practical joke on Gary, but I needed Mr. B's help. I asked him to help me set up the joke and then I'd make sure it was played out once we got to the lake several miles from our camp. Knowing Mr. B was a practical joker, I knew he would be in on the joke right away as well as John, since John always helped out with my jokes.

It was the day before we planned on hiking to the lake when Mr. B asked if John and I were going to take Gary up to the mountain lake above our camp. I said we had planned on heading there the next day. At this point Mr. B told Gary about the tradition of carving your initials into a large rock and placing this rock on a pile of other rocks at the lake. He said he started this tradition several years ago and even mentioned he saw the pile of rocks the last time he was there. He also pointed at me and said he remembered when I took my rock to the top and how small it was compared to the others. (That was meant as a joke on me.) Mr. B went on to say the pile now stands about four feet tall due to the amount of rocks others have carried to this lake, and he was wondering if Gary was going to carry on the tradition.

Mr. B also said that each new hiker tries to outdo the others by finding the biggest rock he can carry and then try to balance the rock on top of the pile once he gets it to the lake to show off his abilities. No small rocks are allowed, he said. He went on to tell Gary he needed to find a fairly good size rock today and to carve his initials in it before he made the trek tomorrow, since carving into a rock found at the lake was not allowed. Once he found a rock Mr. B said he had to approve the size since he was the one who started the tradition and he wouldn't allow any more puny rocks to be placed on the pile like I had done. (Again, another slam at me.) Once the size of the rock was approved, Mr. B instructed Gary on how he should carve his initials into the rock with his knife or some other metal object. The initials had to be deep and large enough so they could be read years from now when others brought their rocks to the pile.

It didn't take long for Gary to find a large rock, about eight to ten pounds in size, and for him to start etching his initials into it. He spent a few hours etching his initials into the rock, and once it met Mr. B's approval he stowed it away in his day-pack for the following day.

The next morning we set out for the lake. It was a hard hike up the hill, especially for Gary who was carrying eight to ten pounds of extra weight in his pack. At one point, while climbing the really steep part of the mountain face, Gary took the rock out of his pack and was about to chuck it off into oblivion. I quickly told him he was almost to the top and to keep the rock in his pack since we were very close.

Soon we reached the top of the mountain and headed to the lake. Gary was excited to get to the lake and to unpack the rock from his day-pack, which he had been carrying for the past couple of hours. Once we got to the lake, he was excited, yet a bit confused. He was looking everywhere for the pile of rocks with initials on them that Mr. B told him about and what he heard John and I confirm. John and I wanted to keep the joke going by leading him around the lake with the rock, but we both started to laugh. That's when Gary caught on that the entire rock thing was a practical joke, he couldn't believe he carved his initials into a rock for no reason and then carried it for three hours up a mountain to a lake where there wasn't a pile of rocks to be found, especially a pile with a bunch of initials etched in them. He was a bit upset at John and me for a while, but he got over it and he was able to share his pain with Mr. B once we returned to Base Camp 1 later that day.

The joke which was played on Gary was basically over, but as for me, another joke was about to be played on me, one that I should have seen coming.

The day after our day hike to the lake, Gary, John, and I set off deeper into the woods. Mr. B and his friends were scheduled to hike out to their cars the same day, which meant they would be out a few days before we were. John, my "rock-carrying" buddy, Gary, and I went deeper into the mountains and explored more trails and lakes. On the day before we hiked out and ended this adventure, we were camped at a lake about sixteen miles from the trailhead where our car was parked.

That afternoon, the day before we were to hike out, we all went through our backpacks getting them ready for our hike out. John and I had our backpacks all set, and Gary was still messing around with his when John asked if anyone wanted to join him for a swim. John wanted to swim to a small island just a few hundred feet off shore. I decided to go for it while Gary, my "rock-carrying" friend, said he was going to stay back in camp and finish getting his backpack in order. What I really think Gary meant to say was that he was going to get my backpack in order.

So while John and I were swimming to the island in the middle of the lake, Gary definitely had other activities planned. What Gary needed was this time to unpack my backpack and place a very large rock in the bottom of it. Now, Gary didn't just toss the monstrosity of a boulder in my backpack, he carefully wrapped it up in some of my clothes and placed it neatly back into the bottom of my backpack. He then reloaded my backpack in the exact manner I had packed it earlier that day. Gary knew I wouldn't unpack it again since we all said we were getting our packs ready for the next morning so we could break camp as early as possible and hike out before the heat of the day. John and I finished our swim, and later that night we all sat around talking about our past several days and the fun we had, even Gary laughed about the rock he carried to the top of a mountain.

The next morning it was time to break camp, and as usual I was eager to get going. I knew what was ahead of us and the amount of miles we were about to hike, not to mention the terrain wasn't a nice flat trail, it's up and down several mountains and across a couple of rivers. So when I put the pack on my back that morning, I didn't realize my friend Gary, the "rock-carrying" buddy I knew, had added a few extra pounds in my backpack. I was either too eager to hit the trail and get to my car, or I was just oblivious to the weight and thought I must have not slept well the night before. So on went the backpack and off we went. We hiked the sixteen miles without a peep about the rock in my backpack.

Once we got to where our car was supposed to be, we found my car nowhere to be found. So I hiked (without my backpack) three more additional miles down a dirt road to a place I knew there was a phone. I called Mr. B to see where my car was, and he told me a porcupine had eaten the break lines and other hoses on his car and the same porcupine must have eaten my break lines too. Mr. B knew where my keys were, so he drove my car to a shop in hopes of getting it fixed before we hiked out. Unfortunately, it was not fixed yet and this was not a joke. A friend of Mr. B picked us up in his pickup truck, and we waited until the following day to get my car. Note of wisdom: Be aware of car-eating porcupines, they can do some damage.

After getting my car the following day, we drove the twelve hours back to Arizona. I was extremely tired, so I dumped my backpack onto my garage floor and waited until the next day to unload and clean it all out. It was then, and only then, when I discovered this very large rock at the bottom of my pack. It was wrapped up in some of my clothes, and I knew in an instant who to blame, my "rock-carrying" friend, Gary. When he answered the phone he just started to laugh, he laughed so hard he couldn't carry on a conversation on the phone.

A few days later we saw each other and we both laughed about each of us carrying a rock for miles. He said he felt really bad (for only a brief moment) when he saw me carry a rock for the sixteen plus miles and then watch me walk away to hike another three miles to get someone to pick us up. I remember my back was killing me and my knees have never been the same. From now on I'll think twice before playing the "Can I have your initials please?" joke on my friends and will always check my backpack before I lug it out of camp.

To this day I am not 100 percent sure if my good ole' buddy John was in on the joke when he asked that day at the lake if anyone wanted to go for a swim. Asking us to go swimming with Gary declining to do so made sense, it was a perfect distraction for Gary to place the rock in my backpack while John and I were out for a swim, that's what I would have done. I only wish I would have thought of it prior to carrying that darn rock so far.

I had the rock Gary gave me on one of my book shelves for years, and every time I looked at the rock I would laugh and think about the trick I played on Gary and the one he played on me. One day I hope I can find out if John was in on this joke. He probably was!

Chapter 7

Hey, You in the Camp!

Imagine being on a backpacking trip miles away from anywhere in particular with a few friends. The days are quite, the last person who was seen was miles away on some remote trail. At night everyone is able to sleep out under the stars, and then one night, right before everyone climbs into his sleeping bag for a good night snooze, someone in the group hears a voice off in the distance yelling and making threats. They hear a deep and menacing voice saying he will sneak into the camp and take all the food and cooking supplies while everyone is asleep. For days nobody has seen a sole in the area, and it is understood that the camp is miles away from any established trail or camping area. The voice off in the distance brings a feeling that someone has been spying on everyone in camp for possibly a day or two.

That's kind of creepy, isn't it? Well, hold on to see how this joke actually played out.

John and I have been taking groups on backpacking trips now for several years, sometimes with people who have been with us before and sometimes with a mixed group of newbies and old-timers. This year we had two of our friends join us who had never been backpacking with us before. Since I knew these guys for years, I had a sneaky feeling they had heard almost all of the practical jokes John and I had played on others, I figured I'd take a break this year. Then about a month prior to the trip, one of the guys asked if he could bring his teenage nephew and one of his friends on the trip, both were about fourteen years old. We had plenty of room and adding two more to the group wasn't a problem, so John and I both agreed. This however changed the joke dynamic. I always enjoyed having fresh blood to play practical jokes on, so I knew I had to plan something big, something our two other friends had never heard of, and something these teenagers would never expect. They were perfect prey for a good practical joke.

My mind started to plan out a practical joke that nobody would expect, one that would cause a little fear, but one that would get some really good laughs after it was all said and done, and hopefully our friendships would be stronger because of it.

The Setup

In order for this joke to work, it is important to find a quality small tape recorder with a set of fairly good portable speakers. (Remember, these items must be carried in a backpack for miles, so don't bring a giant boom box or huge speakers. They need to be lightweight and able to be secretly packed into a backpack.) The speakers need to be able to project a good sound at least thirty yards without sounding distorted or muted; the sound needs to be as clear, as loud, and as real as possible.

At first I was thinking of recording a wild animal, but the problem with this idea was that a wild animal would move about and not stay in one location once it started to make sounds. I couldn't move the speakers and tape recorder once it started to play the recording, so I had to think of something or someone who would typically stay in a stationary location. This led me to the decision to make the recording of a person yelling at us, demanding something from us, or at least making some threats toward us as the tape would play. I knew I would have to write a script and find a person with a deep menacing voice to record. The voice had to be clear enough and loud enough to play out this joke. Luckily John and I had a friend who had the perfect voice and enjoyed playing jokes on others just as much as we did, so he agreed to help be the "voice in the distance."

The script I wrote was based on us being at Base Camp 1 for a couple of nights and allowing John and me time to tell the story of the practical joke "Hey, Mr. Ranger" that Mr. B played on us several years prior. This would allow us to introduce the name of Mr. B and set the stage for what I hoped would work with the recording and the script.

After the script was done, I met with my friend with the deep voice and we recorded his side of the conversation. I first hit the record button, and we recorded nothing for about five minutes. This would give me time once in camp to hit the play button and get back to camp in plenty of time before the voice would yell out at us. As the tape continued to record, my friend would say his line then allow a thirty-second to a minute-long segment where nothing was being recorded as the tape continued on. These segments where nothing was being recorded, or where there was nothing being said, gave me time to talk back to the voice as if I was carrying on a conversation. If it were laid out on paper it would look like this:

- Five minutes of no sound
- Menacing voice
- Thirty to sixty seconds of no sound
- Menacing voice
- Thirty to sixty seconds of no sound
- Menacing voice
- Thirty to sixty seconds of no sound
- Menacing voice

Once the recording was done, I rehearsed what I would say during the thirty to sixty seconds where there was no sound coming from the tape as if I was having a conversation with this lone voice in the darkness. I told John what my plan was and that I needed his help when we were at Base Camp 1 to make it seem more realistic. Of course John was all about making the joke play out, and he did an amazing job. I rehearsed the entire dialog I would have with the recorded voice over and over again so I knew every line and every word I would say back to the menacing voice in the darkness when it was my turn to speak. If it worked, the scary night would be something we would all remember and would be an awesome story to tell later down the road.

The Joke: Hey, You in the Camp!
Location: Base Camp 1

After hiking the grueling miles to get to Base Camp 1, and after being there for a couple of nights, we were all getting very comfortable with the camp and its surroundings. Everyone was so comfortable with the surroundings and the openness of Base Camp 1 that they all wanted to sleep out on the granite and look at the stars. The teenage boys decided to place their sleeping bags about thirty yards away from the main camp, higher up the granite slopes, and in a spot where there was soft sand and plenty of room to lay their sleeping pads and bags down without fear of rolling down the hill. The other guys had their pads and bags laid out elsewhere, all within a thirty-yard radius from the main campsite. Basically, everyone had his sleeping bag spread out all over the granite landscape of Base Camp 1 far away from each other.

With our sleeping bags laid out around the campsite, everyone regrouped and sat around the campfire to talk about the day's events and what the plans were for the next few days. As it was just starting to get nice and dark, John and I decided to tell the story of how Mr. B played the "Hey, Mr. Ranger" joke on us as told in chapter 3. As we sat there telling the story, we made sure to keep addressing the fact that we never saw anyone around Base Camp 1 and the night Mr. B and his pranksters came into our camp was a night just like the one we were experiencing that evening. The sky was clear, there was no moon, and it was just as dark as it was then.

The "Hey, Mr. Ranger" joke brought a lot of laughs once again, and we were all just having a good time talking about it and other adventures John and I have had backpacking around the area. After a few more minutes I pretended to get up and head off into the darkness to relieve myself, or at least that's what I wanted everyone to think I was doing. I made sure nobody was really paying too much attention to me while I grabbed my tape recorder and the speakers I had in my backpack for the last several days. I hid them under my jacket and headed up the granite out of sight, but definitely in earshot of everyone in camp. Once everything was set up, I was ready to give the performance of my life, between me and a recorded voice, to some friends and hopefully some freaked out teenage boys.

I set up the recorder and the speakers then hit play. The recorder was on, and I knew I had about five minutes to get back to camp before the menacing voice started to yell at us. I made it back into camp with plenty of time, I actually was wondering if the recorder was going when all of a sudden the voice from the dark yelled out. The following is how the recording and the "Hey, you in the camp!" joke went.

Now that I was back in camp, I sat down with the rest of the gang as I did. I told them that while I was out taking a pee, I thought I heard something off in the distance and thought I saw a flashlight or something. Everyone just blew it off and went back to looking at the fire. Then, suddenly a voice was heard in the distance, but I pretended not to hear it. The performance was on!

The menacing voice yelled, "Hey, you in the camp!"

(Nothing was recorded on the tape so I had time to see if anyone could actually hear the voice and respond.)

One of the boys sitting near me said, "Did you hear that? It sounded like someone was yelling at us," at which point I replied, "I didn't hear anything, are you sure?"

Then the voice in the distance yelled out, "Hey! I'm talking to you in the camp! (Thirty to sixty second pause on the tape with nothing being broadcasted on the speakers.)

The boys heard the voice again, and so did everyone else. I said to the group, "It sounds like Mr. B.? I wonder if he's trying to play a joke on us. Maybe it was his flashlight I saw."

The menacing voice played again, "Hey, I know you can hear me, I can see ya all looking at me and I saw that guy taking a piss a minute ago." (Again, nothing was recorded on the tape, so I had time to speak.)

This was the time when I started to yell back to the voice in the dark.

My response back to the recorder was, "Is that you, Mr. B? Are you trying to play another one of your jokes on us?"

Menacing voice yelled, "It ain't Mr. B, and it don't matter who it is, and this ain't no joke!"

My response back to the recorder was, "Well, what do you want and why don't you come on down here into camp?"

Menacing voice said, "What I want? I want your food and your cooking stuff! Bring it up here and leave it, I'll get it later. If I come down there you ain't gonna like what's gonna happen!"

I responded back to the recorder, "You want what? Are you saying you're going to try to take our stuff?"

The menacing voice said, "I aint gonna try, I'm gonna get your food and your cooking stuff! Now bring it up here and leave it by these here sleeping bags, I'll be watching and I'll get it later."

My response back to the recorder was, "You're crazy! We're not bringing anything up there."

The menacing voice said, "You think I'm crazy? Then try this."

At this point in time John was standing behind everyone who was fixated looking up hill toward the menacing voice in the dark. Everyone had a flashlight on and were scanning the granite hills trying to see the person with the mysterious voice and figure out where it was coming from. While we were all shining our flashlights up the hill toward the voice in the dark, John secretly started tossing rocks almost straight up into the air and a little toward the voice. As he tossed these rocks into the air, the rocks would land about fifteen feet in front of the group and then come bouncing down toward everyone's feet. (Since the area where the rocks were landing was uphill from our camp, gravity took over and the rocks naturally came bouncing into our camp as if somebody uphill was actually throwing rocks at us.) Even though I knew John was tossing the rocks behind our backs, it actually felt like someone was throwing rocks at us from where the voice was coming from. It was awesome!

As the rocks came rolling into our camp, it was my turn to speak out. "Hey, quit throwing rocks at us, if you want something come on down here and get it, show yourself and maybe we could help you out."

The menacing voice yelled, "I don't want your help, I just want your food and your cooking stuff!

My response back to the recorder was, "Do you have a gun, because that's the only way you're getting our food, you'll have to take it from us."

The menacing voice said, "No problem, I'll get it from you one way or another and I ain't gonna tell ya if I have a gun or not, you'll just have to find out! You've got five minutes to decided, if I don't see ya bringing your stuff up here, I'll come down there and get it when you're all asleep."

This was the last time we would hear from the menacing voice since it was the end of the recording.

Even though both John and I knew the tape recording was over, we continued to yell a few other choice things at the recorder while the others stood by waiting for a response from the mysterious voice. After hearing no response from the crazy person, John said to the group that we should go look for this guy.

Everyone was still standing by the campfire looking up the granite hill trying to use flashlights to see if they could catch a glimpse of the person who was tossing rocks at us and threatening to take our food. Nobody saw anything and nobody gave it a thought to go hunt this crazy person down, except John. John was using his flashlight to scan the area too, but what was great about John, he was so convincing that when he pretended to see someone up the hill from our campsite, the others in our group thought they actually saw someone too. Then John, without a word, bolted off into the darkness as if he was going to find the guy who was tossing the rocks at us and demanding our food supply. As John ran off to catch the guy who was making these threats, the two teenage boys got freaked out and yelled to him not to go. Within seconds John was out of sight.

A few minutes later, out from the vast darkness came some more rocks down the granite hillside, and then we heard John yell, "I see you," as if he actually saw the crazy guy tossing the rocks at us. John then yelled to the rest of us, who were still standing by the campfire, "Come on, guys, he's right over here!" This caused me to run up the hill to help John out and get the others to do the same thing. Of course I headed right to the speakers and tape recorder so

I could hide them before anyone else found them. I knew if the boys found the recorder and speakers, the joke would be over.

The others hesitated for a couple of minutes back in camp, but soon got involved with the man hunt. As I stashed the goods, I yelled to John that I saw him head toward the sleeping bags where the boys had set up their stuff for the night. We both ran toward their bags and pretended to see the guy run up the hill further away from camp. The search for this guy went on for a long time. We actually had everyone in our camp running around the granite hills of Base Camp 1 with flashlights looking for someone who didn't exist. The two guys and the two teenage boys all believed there was some crazy guy out there who wanted our food and that this crazy person would wait until we were all asleep to get it.

We spent most of the night looking for this voice and any signs of this guy coming near our camp. John, at one point, pointed out a set of footprints he found and was able to convince the boys these prints were from the guy we were looking for, when in fact they were one of our own prints we made earlier that day or possibly even that night. The footprints made the person seem even more real and even scarier since we now had proof he was really out there watching us. As anyone in this situation could imagine, everyone in the group was a bit nervous about this crazy person watching us and nobody wanted to sleep out among the granite hills as they had planned earlier that day.

As it got later into the night, the hunt for this crazy person came to an end and we decided to call it quits. We decided to set up a night watch to ensure this voice in the darkness wouldn't take us by surprise and sneak into our camp. John said he would take the first watch, and I agreed to take the second. The boys however didn't want any part of being up alone, so they suggested the other two guys in our group take the later night watches. As we all agreed to how the night was going to go, the boys decided they didn't like the fact their sleeping bags and gear were up in the granite hills where this crazy person might still be spying on us. They soon asked someone to go with them to gather their sleeping gear and bring it back into camp. The others who had their sleeping bags scattered elsewhere along the granite hills also gathered their stuff and brought it back into the camp area since there was safety in numbers. Soon all the sleeping bags were lined up side-by-side in camp as if all of them were attached to each other (they weren't, but it sure did feel like they were). We gathered all the food and cooking supplies and stored them at our feet in a very secure and safe location so this crazy person wouldn't be able to sneak in our camp and grab it from us.

We all started to climb into our sleeping bags when all of a sudden I had to go relieve myself again, at least that's what I told everyone I was going to do. I grabbed my flashlight and off I went back up the hill where the crazy, menacing, deep voice was coming from. I soon retrieved my recorder and speakers and headed back to the campfire. As I walked back to camp I turned the volume down on the recorder and rewound the tape to the beginning where the voice said for the first time, "Hey, you in the camp!" When I got back to camp everyone was in their sleeping bag and everyone was talking softly about the crazy guy, someone asked if I saw anything while I was out taking care of business. I told them I didn't see or hear anything.

Soon it was nice and dark at camp, the campfire was just a soft glow and everyone seemed to be looking at the stars above wondering where this crazy person was right now. Because they weren't paying any attention to me, I was able to climb into my sleeping bag with the speakers and the recorder by my side and just lay there a few minutes listening to the silence of the night and the occasional question of, "Do you think that guy can see us now, now that the fire is out?" John, who was our first night watchman, assured us everything was okay and not to worry.

After about ten minutes of nothing being said and only silence in the air, I decided to hit the "play" button on my recorder.

Within minutes, the deep, menacing voice came out of my sleeping bag saying, "Hey, you in the camp!" and as soon as the voice came out of my sleeping bag, everyone knew they had been on the receiving end of one of our practical jokes. They all took a few hits at my sleeping bag with me in it, but it was worth the punishment to hear them laugh about how we got them to believe there was a crazy guy out in the hills wanting our stuff and that we were able to get them all chasing around the hills of Base Camp 1 looking for someone that didn't exist.

Even though we all knew the voice in the darkness was a joke, the sleeping conditions didn't change much that night and the boys never did sleep up on the hill in their cool sandy location away from everyone else.

Just remember this story the next time strange sounds are heard coming from the hills or woods around camp, it could be the real deal or it could be some crazy nut like me playing a joke on some unsuspecting friends.

Chapter 8

Do You Really Want to Follow the Leader?

Have you ever been asked to follow someone on a trip? Maybe you've been the person that others are following. Either way, following the leader can sometimes be funny if you are the leader or you know exactly where the leader is going. Sitting back and watching others follow without any clue where they are going can be entertaining.

Over the years of backpacking, I've had the experience of taking several people on trips deep into the mountains and wondered what would happen if something bad happened to me. Could those who trusted me be able to find their way back to our cars and get help, or would we all die deep in the woods of northern California? Typically I would ask the guys who were new to backpacking if they knew how to use their map and if they could find their way out. A lot of times I didn't have to worry since my friend John was on these trips, but several years ago John retired and moved on to seek new adventures. Even with John's moving on, I continued to take guys on backpacking trips. One year I put my fears to the test to see if the guys who trusted me could find their way out. Here's how the story went and the joke that came known as "Following the Leader."

The Setup

There is no setup for this joke to take place, all you need is to have people who trust you and think you know where you are going. It helps if you have an area picked out to lead your followers to and around.

The Joke: Following the Leader
Location: On the trail or even while driving a car; as long as friends are following close behind.

A few years ago there were about five other guys on a backpacking trip with me. John had since moved away, and I was the guy in charge of the safety and wellbeing of the group. On this particular trip, none of the guys who were with me had ever been backpacking with me before, nor did they know the area like I did or where we were hiking. They were all trusting me to get them home safe and sound while at the same time show them some amazing country.

We had already hiked and set up camp in a spot several miles north of Base Camp 1 when one day I asked the guys if they wanted to go on a day hike to another lake I knew of to the east of us. I told them the hike would be about a two hour hike and there is no trail to get there. They all agreed, so off we went.

Since I knew where the lake was and since nobody had ever been to it before, I naturally took the lead. We hiked for about an hour or two when we finally got to the lake. We hung out, went swimming, had lunch, and just relaxed for most of the afternoon when we decided to head back to our campsite. Again I took the lead back to our campsite since there wasn't a trail from the lake to our camp, nor did we leave any good indicators how to get back to camp either. As we walked along, I noticed the guys behind me were fairly close on my heels and not paying too much attention to their surroundings. It was then that I decided to see how blind their trust was in me as the leader. As I walked along leading this group of carefree guys, I saw a large grouping of tall pine trees ahead of me and decided to set my plan into action. The trees were in a fairly large grouping or circle, the grouping was approximately thirty feet in diameter with large brush on the edges of it and an easy flat surface to walk around it. As we headed for these trees, the guys were still close behind me and still weren't paying attention to their surroundings. I proceeded to walk around the grouping of trees not saying anything, just walking around the trees. It was about the third time making the entire circle when one of the guys said, "Hey, I think we've walked past these trees before." I started to laugh and said, we've walked around these trees almost three times already and I was beginning to worry how many more times we would walk around them before anyone spoke up. We all laughed a bit more before heading back. They learned how easy it was to follow someone without thinking about where they were going.

That evening back at camp, I sat and thought about how difficult it was to get to our campsite and wondered if anyone paid attention to the trail markers I set up and where the trail was in the first place when we were hiking in. This question started to bug me, so I asked the guys if any of them would be able to find their way out if I got seriously injured or possibly died back here. Of course they all said yes, so I said I would put them to the test on the day we were to hike back to our cars. I told them I would bring up the rear of the group as we hiked out. The person in front would lead us out, and if they took the wrong trail or path I would allow the others to follow him down the wrong trail a bit and before informing the group they were all lost and are now dead. After the first person leads us down the wrong path I would put the next person in line at the front of the pack and wait to see if they too would lead us down the wrong trail and to our deaths.

A day or so later we were all set to hike out and back to our cars when I asked who wanted to be the leader and start our journey back to our cars. One of the guys said he could get us out with no problem, so he took the lead. I actually thought this guy could pull it off since he had been hiking around our camp for the past couple of days checking everything out making sure he knew exactly which way to go. As we put on our backpacks for the sixteen-mile hike out, he started to lead the group. Unfortunately for him, it only took a few minutes before he was leading the group down a game trail which headed off in the totally opposite direction. I stopped where he and the rest of the group took the wrong turn and waited a few minutes before I yelled to my band of lost backpacker they were all lost and now presumed dead. When they all turned around and headed back to my location, I showed them the trail and then said to the guy who was leading the group, "You killed us all, back to the end of the line for you." After I took the leader and put him behind me, I let the next person in line start leading the group, I even allowed others to give him advice as we hit points along the trail, which were confusing to those who didn't know which way to go. Soon he too would be heading down the wrong path in completely the wrong direction, and again I would say, "You are all lost and are all dead." This went on for a good couple of hours and several miles. I think we went through the line at least two or three times before I took over the lead and got these guys out.

The first part of this story was a small joke of following the leader, the second part was more of a warning for those following someone into the mountains or woods and not paying attention to their surroundings. It's okay to follow the leader, just make sure they aren't taking you around in circles in the process.

Another similar story, but not while hiking in the woods, took place when I was the lead car of a small group of three other cars heading to a water park with a bunch of kids. As we drove toward the water park, one of the other drivers asked if I knew of a place to eat where the kids would enjoy the food. I told them of a place at a nearby shopping center. All the other drivers agreed to follow me, and so I took the lead. As we drove I noticed the other cars were fairly close behind me, at times so close that if I had to slam on my breaks they would be in my car with me. Once we got near the shopping center I decided to see how trustworthy the other drivers were of my knowledge of where I was going. I pulled into this huge parking lot at the shopping center where no other cars were parked. I then drove all over the parking lot in a zigzag pattern and even around in a huge circle. The kids who were in my car while I drove all over the place were laughing so hard because it was funny to watch the other drivers just blindly following me wherever I went. The only person who didn't laugh was the security guard of the shopping center who thought we were all out for a joyride when he pulled me over to see if I needed any help with directions.

When being the leader of a group, have fun, but remind those who are following you they should pay a little more attention when being lead somewhere they've never been before. Now, if you're the one following someone else, pay attention to see if they are actually leading you or they are just taking you on a joyride.

Chapter 9

Is that a USFS Message Container?

Have you ever wondered how someone in the back country, miles away from any civilization, without a cell phone or Internet service, gets information about forest fires in their area or impending doom? Well, don't fear, your friendly message container is here! At least that's what we told one group of guys who went backpacking with us.

A couple of years prior to playing this joke, we were camping at Base Camp 1 getting ready to hike toward Camp 3 when we noticed a huge column of smoke about twenty to thirty miles away. The smoke clearly indicated there was a forest fire miles away from us, but we weren't sure if it was near Camp 3 or if it would possibly shift and head toward our direction. These questions could not be answered, so we decided not to hike to Camp 3 like we had planned and instead hike to a different lake we enjoyed in the past. While camping at the other lake, which was miles in the opposite direction, but still in an area where we could see the huge column of smoke, we wondered how someone would know about forest fires in the area other than seeing smoke like we did and how would they know what to do or what areas to stay away from if nobody told them what was going on. That's when this idea came to me for a really funny practical joke.

In the past, while at Base Camp 1, John and I have seen military jets and service helicopters once in a while fly low to the ground and up the granite canyons on drills or possibly training missions to fly stealthier through canyons and mountainous terrain. Either way, I thought, what if the helicopters or maybe even a small fixed wing airplane could fly over areas where they knew people were camping and drop a message container with information in it. As I sat there pondering this possibility, my mind went the other way and thought, what if I could make someone believe the forestry service actually developed message containers to drop on backpackers when people in the back country needed to be notified of a possible hazard such as forest fires, or possibly a rouge bear; and who could I play this joke on? I knew the forest service required permits to hike in most areas, so it made sense that they could feasibly know where most of the back country hikers are and easily drop message containers on their campsites when needed.

The idea was now established, and soon my practical joking mind took off. The "Message Container" would be developed and played out the next time I'd go backpacking.

The Setup

I had to build a container that would actually work if it was tossed out of a helicopter or small fixed wing airplane. It had to be durable and able to handle a good impact if it hit the ground, so I decided to build a container out of PVC pipe and have it attached to parachute, which was about six feet in diameter.

I had to use a piece of two-inch-diameter PVC pipe to make the container with two PVC caps at each end. The pipe was about ten inches long and a perfect size to slip all kinds of notes or warnings. I painted the container *Forest Service Green* for a reason which I will explain later. I should have painted it a florescent orange color so it could be found easier, but being painted green made the joke even better.

As for the parachute, I'm not good at sewing things, so I had to find someone who had these skills to help me make my parachute. The perfect person was my mother-in-law; she was awesome and seemed to enjoy the fact she was involved in one of my practical jokes. Over the years I've told her many of the jokes I've played in the past, and this time she got to be involved in the initial phase of the joke—building the actual prop.

Once I had the container figured out and the parachute made, I knew I had to make the outside of the container look convincing enough to be an actual message container, one that someone would at least believe it was anyway. Since I had a background in drafting and graphic design, I sat down and designed a sticker to place on PVC pipe. The sticker looked something like this:

 United States Forestry Service
U.S.F.S.
Message Container
Important Message Inside

Please follow all instructions within the container
Return container to nearest Forest Service Station
For A $5.00 Redemption Fee

The following is a detailed list of what is needed to construct the message container:

A) A two-inch-diameter piece of PVC pipe approximately ten inches long and two end caps.
B) PVC pipe glue is only used to glue the cap, which is attached to the parachute and the pipe. Do not glue the bottom cap. Once the pipe is painted, the bottom cap will be a tight fit and no glue is necessary; besides, the container must have a way to be opened.
C) Two cans of spray paint
  a. A florescent color orange would be best, but I used forest green as part of my joke since one of the guys who was going on the trip had issues with the government and the way they do things. The green would just piss him off, and that was awesome to see.
  b. A can of black spray paint to create the initials on the parachute itself.

D) A 6'0" diameter piece of cloth, preferably something that resembles material used in making parachutes and is a bright color if possible. Again, I used a forest green due to guy who had issues with the government and it would make the joke that much better.

E) At least eight (8) eight sections of 4'0" long pieces of para-cord
    a. Secure one end of each section to the parachute by sewing them into place.
    b. Secure the opposite ends of the para-cord to the top cap of the container by drilling a hole large enough to run all eight (8) ends of the para-cord through the top cap and tying the ends to each other on the inside of the cap. I used some silicone around the inside of the cap and at the ends of the para-cord to make the container seem water tight.

F) Sticky back paper or something that a sticker can be made on

G) A printer to print out materials to place inside the message container

H) Large stencils to print letters onto the parachute

I) Items from the forestry service such as campfire regulations, camping restrictions, miscellaneous items about the area, and whatever else that will make the joke more realistic.

J) Last but not least there has to be a convincing letter written to place in the message container that causes the people who are reading it to believe there is a problem or a reason why everyone needs to evacuate camp.

I asked John to help me with the letter, and between the two of us we came up with an idea of a rogue bear; one that was terrorizing backpackers in areas where we planned on hiking to and camping at over the next few days of our trip. John took the lead on the letter and went the extra mile to develop it for this joke. He contacted the forestry department in the area we typically go hiking and asked them for a copy of their letter head. He told them about the joke we were developing and the idea of our message container, they had no problem sending him a copy of their letterhead and other paraphernalia to stuff in the container. These extra items helped make our message container feel like it was the real thing.

The following is an example of what our message container looked like.

At the end of this chapter is a larger diagram of the message container and a facsimile of the letter, which was inserted into the container.

The Joke: Is that a Message Container?
Location: At camp before heading out to a new destination

This trip included six of us. There was John and me and our friends, Greg, Eddy, Billy, and Rob. We took two days to get to Base Camp 1 this year since one of our guys needed some extra time to rest before we headed up to Camp 3, which actually helped this joke work even better.

After spending a day at Base Camp 1, I took Greg, Eddy, and Billy on a day hike while John and Rob stayed back in camp. John told the rest of the group he had been to the lake several times before and wanted to kick back at Base Camp 1 and relax before hiking to Camp 3 the next day. Rob decided he too wanted to stay back at camp and relax. As for the rest of the gang, we headed out for a day hike to the lake I typically would take new people to every year. It's the same lake where we played the "Your Initials Please" rock joke on my friend Gary a few years prior. We left around nine in the morning and figured we would be back around two in the afternoon. The hike took us an hour longer to complete since we walked around the entire lake and followed the creek which ran from it to the river below; the same river that flowed through Base Camp 1 as it descended down the granite canyons.

Where the river and the creek meet was about two miles or so down river from Base Camp 1, and as we were hiking up the river toward Base Camp 1 we ran into Rob. Since I was leading the group, I saw Rob first and made my way to him before the rest of the gang caught up to us. Rob quickly told me John had spilled the beans about the message container joke and had asked him to join in on the fun and not let anyone know it was a joke. I thought John was brilliant in asking Rob to join in on the joke, especially since John had to plant the "message container" up in a tree and probably needed Rob's help to do it while we were out for our day hike. By getting Rob to join in on the fun it provided a better story coming from Rob rather from John or me since Rob had never been backpacking with us before and Rob was new to the group as all the others. Rob made the joke that much more believable.

When I met up with Rob and he told me he knew, I asked him to do me a favor. I asked him to ask the other guys, once they caught up to us, if they had seen the helicopter fly by earlier that day. So, sure enough, the other guys soon caught up to Rob and me, and soon Rob was asking how we were all doing, what was the lake like, and more importantly he asked, "Did you guys see the helicopter fly by an hour or so ago?" Since there was no helicopter none of us said we had seen one, but to my surprise and delight, one of the guys said he thought he heard a helicopter earlier that day. When I heard this, I too pretended I heard the helicopter since I needed the rest of the group to believe an actual helicopter did fly by earlier that day. Soon everyone thought they had heard a helicopter, and so the stage was set.

Once Rob asked us about the helicopter, it opened the door for me to set the hook even further on these unsuspecting soles.

As we were hiking back to Base Camp I told the following tale:

> It was several years ago when John and I, along with a couple of other guys, saw a large column of smoke off in the distance, it seemed to be about twenty miles or so away. We were afraid of it being a large forest fire, one that would cause us to hike out early or possibly cause other issues for our backpacking trip. Early one morning, as we were sitting at Base Camp 1, a helicopter came flying down the canyon and soon was hovering over our campsite. We looked up and someone in the helicopter dropped a small container made out of PVC pipe, which was attached to a parachute. The PVC pipe was something they called a warning container or something like that. In the container it informed us of the forest fire we saw off in the distance and where they, the forest service, predicted the fire might spread to in the next several hours and days, depending on the weather. We wondered how the helicopter crew knew where we were located, so when we hiked out that year we stopped by the forest ranger station where we got our permits, just like we do every year, and we asked the ranger how they knew where to drop the container. The ranger said they track all the permits that are filed, and they have a fairly good idea where and when people will be in certain areas and if people are

in areas of concern. Based on the permits they have a fairly good idea where to drop off these containers. The message in the container they dropped on us said the fire was in the northern part of Yosemite National Park and it posed a threat to those who intend to hike anywhere near this area. This caused John and me to change our plans and hike to a different lake instead of Camp 3 like we planned on doing. We haven't seen anything like this for the past several years and always thought if we would ever see it again.

After I told this little story I asked Rob if he had seen the helicopter drop anything out of it today. Rob said he didn't think so, and so we all kept hiking back to Base Camp 1.

When we got to camp, John was waiting there for us kicking back by the edge of the river reading a book and just relaxing. As some of the guys got in earshot of John, he asked if we saw the helicopter fly by. John soon started the same story as I told since we had both rehearsed it several times. I made sure to stay away from John as he told the same story to the rest of the group so it would seem that much more believable. After a few minutes I walked over to where everyone was hanging out and asked John if he saw the helicopter drop anything out of it. He said he didn't see anything since he woke up from a nap as the helicopter flew by. I said, "Do you think they were on a training mission? I haven't seen any smoke or issues like that where they would drop one of those warning containers, or whatever they call it." He said he didn't think they had dropped anything since he walked around the area and checked to see if they had but soon told the group he didn't find anything.

Later that evening we decided to collect some fire wood before it got dark. John and I directed the group to an area where we knew there was a lot of drift wood and of course where John had hung the message container up in a tree. As we were picking up some of the drift wood, I purposely stood under the message container, which was about five feet above my head, and called to the group to come over and help me with some of the wood I found. As they were walking toward me, Ed saw an object above my head and yelled, "Hey, is that one of those message containers you were talking about?" With that I acted extremely surprised and said it sure does look like one.

We had to find a large branch to get this thing out of the tree. It took us several minutes to get it down, and as soon as we got it down Greg immediately expressed his issues with the government and said, "What the hell, why is this thing green? How do they expect you to find this thing in a forest with green trees?" Greg went on to complain and say they sure are dumb making this thing so un-noticeable. "Why not paint it bright orange and make the parachute more noticeable? This is stupid!" We all agreed of course and only tried to reason why they would do such a dumb thing.

Once we got the container down, I pretended to try to open it from the top. I knew it was glued shut and would not come off, so I handed it to another guy and said, "You try it, I can't get it." I believe I even said maybe the other end might be the way to open it. Sure enough the container opened and out came all sorts of papers and documents. We all sat down and started to go through the items in the container: first was a thing about preventing forest fires, then there was a copy of the rules and regulations of camping in the back country, and finally there was "the letter." The letter looked something like this:

Note: Everything in the letter on the following page is made up, nothing is real about it from the dates, names of the lakes and other locations, and even the phone number was made up. The patch on the upper right corner was taken from the Internet just to give the reader an idea of what the actual letter looked like. Again, *nothing* on this letter is real.

Department of Forestry
U.S.F.S.
800.123.4567

IMPORTANT MESSAGE

DATE: July 25, 1996
LOCATION:

This message is intended for those who plan on hiking to or are currently in the areas listed below.

- Beaver lake
- Crabtree lake
- Crabtree creek
- Elk flats
- Fireside meadows
- Fish Lake
- Horseshoe lake
- Horseshoe creek
- Sunset falls

If you are within 5 miles of these locations you may be affected by the contents of this message.

DIRECTIONS / WARNINGS:

This is a Table 5 bear alert. Over the past several days a rogue bear has been accosting backpackers and destroying their campsites in the areas listed above. The bear is a large brown bear approximately six feet tall when standing on its hind legs and approximately 300 pounds. It has been reported by several backpackers in the above mentioned areas to have destroyed several campsites in search of food and easy prey. Serious injury has occurred to at least 3 backpackers.

Stay away from the above mentioned areas if possible.

If you are currently camping within the above mentioned areas please do the following:

1) Break camp as soon as possible and hike to an area outside the danger zones listed above
2) Ensure your food is properly stored.
   a. Even a bear canister has proven to be unstoppable for this bear
   b. Hang your food between two trees at least 12' above the ground
   c. Do not store items such as tooth paste or items with an odor in your sleeping area

3) Establish someone in your party to stay alert at night since this is when most of the bears' activities have taken place.
4) **DO NOT APPROACH ANY BEARS**

As we read the letter, the guys started to ask if any of the lakes or creeks were anywhere near the area where Camp 3 was located. John and I pulled out our maps of the area where Camp 3 was located and confirmed all the areas listed in the letter were near and around Camp 3. This caused some concern of the group. What was real funny was Greg, the guy who had issues with the government, got really pissed off when he read, "This is a Table 5 Bear Alert." He said, "What the hell is a Table 5 Bear Alert? Who has any clue what this means?" He went on for almost an hour complaining about the message container and how it should have been a bright orange color, and he kept on about what the hell is a Table 5 Bear Alert?

Since the group was a bit concerned about hiking to Camp 3, we sat down after dinner and took a vote. Three guys said nope, we shouldn't go, while Rob, John, and I all voted to go. Since John and I planned the trip and knew we would be responsible for the safety of the group, plus we both knew the way in and out of the area, we were the deciding vote. So the next day we were off to Camp 3 where this rogue bear was supposed to be hanging out accosting backpackers.

The hike to Camp 3 is typically a full days' journey, and most of the time while hiking to Camp 3 we would occasionally meet other backpackers who were enjoying the back country as we were. This hike was no exception. As we hike, John and I would take turns leading the group or bringing up the rear so not to lose anyone in our group as we hiked along. This time I was at the rear of the group hiking along with Ed, one of the guys who didn't want to hike to Camp 3 due to the "Table 5 Bear Alert." Approximately two to three miles before reaching Camp 3, Ed and I came across two guys who were hiking the opposite direction as we were. As we got closer to the guys, I suggested to Ed that maybe these guys might have seen the bear or maybe even were leaving the area because of it, so I suggested to Ed that he might want to ask the guys if they had seen any bears, specifically the bear mentioned in the letter. Here's how it all went down:

I was hiking behind Ed as we approached and stopped to talk to these two guys who were resting along the trail. I'll call them my "helpful backpackers." As we faced the two backpackers, I was able to stand in a spot where Ed was in front of me and couldn't see me, but I was in clear eyesight of the backpackers who could see anything and everything I was doing.

Ed proceeded to ask the guys, "Hey, did you see any bears in your travels?"

As I said, the backpackers had a clear vision of me, so I shook my head up and down saying yes with my mouth but not speaking a word. I also stretched out my arms as far as I could stretch them to indicate they should tell Ed, "Yes, we saw a bear and it was a *huge* one at that."

The helpful backpackers saw me and told Ed exactly what I had hoped for and added even more to the story. They said, "Yep, we saw the bear, it was across the lake from us and up on a ridge. It looked like a huge bear from where they were at."

Ed then asked, "What color was the bear?"

I was lucky enough to be wearing a brown shirt, so I pointed with both hands at my shirt and tugging on it frantically trying to make sure the helpful backpackers would catch on and say, "It was a brownish color." Sure enough these guys were perfect and told Ed exactly that. "It was a golden brown color, maybe a little darker."

Now Ed asked, "Did the bear cause any problems at your camp, or did you hear of any problems with the bear?"

Now I was kind of concerned as to what I should do, especially since the helpful backpackers were looking at me for some sort of direction. All I could do was make a face to indicate the bear was mean, but I had nothing else. But to my surprise, the helpful backpackers said, "We didn't have any issues with bears in our camp, but we talked to a couple of other backpackers who said a bear had gotten into their food supply and destroyed their camp. These guys were camped on the other side of the lake, so that's probably where the bear is now."

Wow, I couldn't have asked for a better story.

We talked to the guys a little longer and soon I said to Ed we better get going because the rest of our group was long gone by now. Soon Ed was heading back on the trail to catch up to the other guys and hopefully telling them what these two backpackers had to say.

I hung back and thanked the two "helpful backpackers" and told them all about the joke we were playing on my friends. They both laughed and said, "With a friend like you, who needs any enemies?" but they also added they can't wait to play the same joke on some of their buddies.

We finally made it to Camp 3 and Ed was in the process of telling the other guys what the helpful backpackers had told him.

While in camp I reminded the guys we needed to hang our food as the letter stated, "12' above the ground and between two trees." What made this so perfect is I knew of a couple of trees near our camp where there were signs of a bear actually scratching the trees. The bear's claw marks were about 5' up the tree trunk and were nice and deep but were very old. John and I noticed the claw marks a couple of years ago, so it was clear they were from a while ago, but that didn't stop me from pointing them out to the guys who were helping me hang the food for the night. This just added more to the suspense.

As we set up our individual tents, I could tell Ed was a bit concerned about the bear since he pitched his tent between John's tent and mine. I guess he felt more protected, or possibly thought he would ensure his safety thinking either John or I would get eaten first before the bear made it to his tent. Either way, it was fairly clear he was concerned. As for the other guys, they didn't seem to show much concern since they pitched their tents elsewhere and one guy even decided to sleep under the stars since it was such a clear night.

The next morning John, Greg, and l went for a hike to check out a couple of lakes, which were a couple of miles away from Camp 3. The other guys just wanted to relax and do some fishing, so off we went. While we were hiking along, Greg asked John and I if we heard anything last night and how well we slept due to the fact the bear could have come into our camp. John and I both said we slept fine and had no concern about the rogue bear. We asked Greg how he slept, and he said he didn't sleep a wink. He said he laid there all night with his big ole' knife in his hand just waiting for the bear to tear through his tent and attack him. The thought of Greg not getting any sleep while at Camp 3 concerned John and me, so we both agreed to tell him the whole "message container" was a joke and the letter inside it was written by John. Greg was about to kill us both right there and then, then asked, "Does anyone else know it's a joke?" I believe he believed he was the only one who didn't know the message container was a joke. So we told him that only Rob knew about it and Ed and Bill still thought it was the real deal. At this point Greg was laughing about it and even commented about the "Table 5 Bear Alert" mentioned in the letter, asking what the heck did that mean. John said he didn't have a clue but it sure did sound important and scary when he wrote it in the letter. He even asked about the parachute and why we used green as the color and not a bright orange?

As we hiked back to Camp 3 we asked Greg to keep the joke a secret until the end of the trip. We wanted to see if Ed or Bill would try to return the fake message container to the ranger station when we hiked out. The container did say to return it to the nearest ranger station for a $5.00 redemption fee.

A couple of days later we were packing up our backpacks for the hike out. I asked if anyone wanted to carry the message container in his backpack. I said that whoever did could claim the $5.00 redemption fee at the ranger station when we stopped to let them know we were out of the back country. Lucky for me, Ed offered to carry it out, so I gladly gave it to him. Once we hiked out, we drove from the trailhead to the ranger station about twenty minutes away. When we got to the ranger station, I told Ed to grab the message container from his backpack, which forced him to unload his backpack to get to it. This gave me plenty of time to run into the ranger station and speak to a ranger who was on duty. I told the ranger of the joke we had played on my friend and asked him if he would like to play along with us when he comes in to return the container and get his $5.00. The ranger said sure, and so I stepped back away from the counter and was looking at some maps on the wall when Ed came walking in with the message container in his hand. He walked over to me and asked who should he talk to. I wasn't sure, so we both went to the counter and the ranger who agreed to help was sitting behind the counter working on his computer when Ed handed him the message container. The ranger took the container, looked at it, and said, "Nice," wrapped the parachute around it and stuffed it under the counter without even looking at Ed or me. The ranger then went back to work on his computer as if nothing had ever happened.

Ed was confused and he looked at me with a look like, "What the heck?" So I said to the ranger, "Excuse me, my friend would like to know about the redemption fee for returning the container." The ranger reached back under the counter, grabbed the container, unwrapped the parachute from around it, read the label again, wrapped the parachute back around the container, and handed it to my friend, Ed, and politely said, "You can keep it," then went back to work on his computer.

Ed was shell shocked. He looked at the ranger, then at the message container, then at me with a look on his face of "What do I do now?" So Ed asked the ranger, "Don't you want this back so you can use it again? And what about the $5.00?"

The ranger then looked up at me, then directly at Ed and said, "You should ask your friend."

Ed then looked at me and said, "Why, what would he know about this?" to which I replied, "This container is not real, I made it and the whole thing is a joke." Ed just shook his head and walked away.

It wasn't until about two hours later, when all of us were eating dinner at a restaurant, that we started to talk about how we planned the entire "Message Container" joke when Ed actually realized the entire rogue bear, "Table 5 Bear Alert" letter, and the message container was all made up. It was like a giant light bulb went off and he said, "Oh my god, that was hilarious!" I believe to this day Ed still has the message container in his possession, and I hope when he looks at it, it brings back fond memories of a backpacking trip he had with a bunch of his friends.

Now, keep in mind, the forestry service might decide to create message containers and drop them from helicopters or small airplanes, however, if they are forestry green in color and the message inside the container doesn't fully explain what a Table 5 Bear Alert is, you can bet your last penny that Ed is playing the joke on you.

Chapter 10

There's a Dead Body in the River

Over the years of playing jokes on our friends, John and I wondered when someone was going to try to pay us back and play a joke on us. It appeared this was the year, the year after we played the "Message Container" joke, with the "rogue bear" letter on our friend Greg. Everyone who was backpacking with us this year had been on previous trips with us in the past, including Greg. Because we knew these guys knew all about our practical jokes, John and I decided not to play any this year.

Then one day, while John and I were playing cards and relaxing at Base Camp 1, a joke was about to be played on us. Well, at least that's what the other guys thought they were going to do. Greg was the ring leader for the group, and he spent a few days and a few dollars on this joke of his. He didn't let the other guys in on the joke until later when he needed help setting everything into place. The only problem was, John and I had a sneaky suspicion he was up to something the day he put his joke into action.

The Setup

First, Greg or anyone planning to play this joke on their friends needs to be over twenty-one, or at least old enough to go into an adult bookstore and purchase a blow-up doll. Greg said he felt like a total pervert walking into an adult bookstore to buy a blow-up doll for this joke, especially when he had to ask the clerk, "Hey, where are your blow-up dolls?" Then he tried to explain to the clerk it wasn't for him, it was for a joke he was going to play on his friends. I'm sure the clerk had heard that story time and time again.

Next, after getting over feeling like a total pervert, the doll needed to be dressed in clothes that could get wet and possibly destroyed in the execution of the practical joke. Then all this stuff, the blow-up doll and the clothes, needed to be packed and hidden in the bottom of a backpack until the time was right.

Finally, once in the back country, an appropriate time needed to be figured out, get the blow-up doll out of the backpack, blow it up to its life-size form, get it dressed in its backpacking attire, and then figure out how to weigh the doll down so it would sink to the bottom of a deep pool without being washed down stream or having those being pranked see any of this. There is a lot going on here.

The Joke: There's a Dead Body in the River
Location: Along a river where it's safe to swim in and has deep pools of water nearby.

The following description of how the joke actually went was from John and my perspective. I'm sure Greg had a different view of the story and how he *totally* made us believe there was a dead body at the bottom of the river.

John and I would typically hang out playing cards in the area we called our kitchen at Base Camp 1 prior to preparing dinner for the rest of the group. From our vantage point we could see up river about a half mile or so and down river about the same distance if not more. There were very few trees to block our view of the river and the massive granite valley it flowed though. Generally speaking, the main view from Base Camp 1 was either upstream or down since on the south side of the camp was the base of a huge granite mountain.

One evening, while we were playing cards we noticed Greg heading upstream with a bag under his arm or something like that. We didn't pay too much attention because almost every evening before dinner Greg would take a stroll upriver. However, this time he was acting a bit suspicious by the way he stopped and looked at us to see if we were watching him. We continued to play cards for about an hour or so. When we were done, we saw Greg doing something upriver almost out of sight of our camp. John and I both looked at each other and asked, "I wonder what Greg is up to." We watched him for about fifteen minutes or so before we noticed he was moving something around in one of the huge pools upriver. We figured he was messing around with something floating in the water, so John and I went back to discussing what we were going to make for dinner and where we planned on hiking to next. Either way, we kind of left Greg to do whatever Greg wanted to do. Others from our group decided to hike up river to see what Greg was up to, but John and I stayed back at camp and relaxed.

It was about thirty minutes later when Greg started to yell at us from his position up river. John and I could hardly hear what he was trying to say because of the sound of the river and his distance away from camp, but based on the way he was jumping up and down and waving his arms we figured he had something important to show us. Others from our group were by his side and they too were waving their arms as if they all were trying to catch John's and my attention. John looked at me and said, "I think Greg is trying to play a joke on us, do you want to go up river and play along with his joke, or do you want to sit here and pretend we didn't see them?" We remembered what we did to him the year before with the "Message Container," so we figured he was out to get us back. As we sat in camp, we both agreed to hike up river and see what the problem was. However, we both decided to take our time walking there and to show no concern if possible.

As John and I were walking up river, which took us about ten minutes to get where everyone was at, we were trying to figure out what the practical joke was going to be: Was it going to be a dead animal floating in the pond with some sort of gross thing oozing out of it, was it going to be a dead body, or possibly some strange object that fell from the sky? Either way, John and I were getting ready to go along with the gag and not appear to have anything bother us.

When we got closer to Greg and his partners in crime, who were all standing around this huge pool of water along the river, they started to yell to us saying they think there is something at the bottom of the pool, possibly "a dead body."

Note: If anyone from our group would have thought there was a dead body at the bottom of a pool, they wouldn't be standing there waiting for John and me to hike to their location. They would have tried to rescue this supposed dead body, but not our band of heroes, they waited for John and me to get there.

As John and I reached the edge of the pool, all of the pranksters continued to point at a strange object at the bottom of the pool and say it looked like a dead body, but both John and I said we doubted it and looked at what appeared to be a dark shadow at the bottom of the pool. We said, "It sure does look like something, but doubt it would be a dead body, let's fish it out and see." Now everyone else was acting all freaked out as if this object was a real person stuck at the bottom of this pool, but John and I just acted like it was nothing big, especially since if it were a dead body. These guys would have gotten it out thirty minutes prior to us finishing our card game, pondering on what was for dinner, and taking a leisurely stroll up the river to where they were all standing by the water's edge, especially with objects around them, which they could have easily fished this thing out of the water way before we got to them.

John and I quickly found a long piece of driftwood near the river's edge and started to use it to fish out the object. We had fun snagging the object, then letting it slip off the driftwood and then snag it again. It took us a good fifteen to twenty minutes to fish this thing out. Each time we let it slip off the driftwood, Greg and his pranksters would ooh and aah and keep on saying, "It looks like a body," one even said it looked like a female. Of course it was, it was a blow-up doll! John and I kept on playing around with these guys by taking our sweet time fishing it out.

Finally John and I got it out of the water, it was obvious it wasn't a person, but the pranksters kept on saying, "It's a dead body, it's a dead body." All John and I found was a drenched blow-up doll from a sex store wearing some old clothes with its feet tied together with some very heavy rocks attached to them. As the dead blow-up doll exited the water, John and I could only say, "Nice try, buddy, thanks for thinking of getting us back, the effort you took to pull this off means a lot to us."

Greg then laughed and told us how hard it was to do this. He told us about going into the adult bookstore and all he did to prepare for the joke, but he said he didn't prepare for how hard it would be to sink this thing to the bottom of the pool. He said it took him forever to blow up the doll, dress it, and then figure out how to sink it to the bottom of the pool without making it look too obvious. He said he had one heck of a time because it kept on wanting to float down river and out of the pool.

After the joke had been played, nobody wanted to put this blow-up doll in his backpack, what would their wives say when they got back home? "What really goes on back there in the woods anyway?" We first laughed about playing a joke on one of our wives, but decided that wouldn't be a good idea, so we decided to destroy it and toss it in the trash once we got back to our cars and to a dumpster.

What John and I thought about this joke was that we are glad to have friends who would go to this much trouble to get back at us for a joke we played on them. We always knew a joke could always be played on us and we almost always expected it, we just didn't expect the joke to involve a blow-up doll from an adult sex store.

Chapter 11

Let's Chase That Shadow!

When camping at Base Camp 1, the sun typically starts to set around seven thirty in the evening during the month of July. As the sun would set, it would slowly disappear behind a vast mountain range to the west of camp. As the sun would go down, Base Camp 1 would be greeted by the mountain's shadow. The shadow would then slowly climb the granite mountain to the east of Base Camp 1 and keep climbing it until darkness fell upon our camp. The mountain to the east of camp rose about 800 to 900 feet above camp and was a bit steep in several locations. Typically when the sun hit the top of this mountain, we would light our campfire for the night. This particular year we got to watch not only the shadow climb the mountain, but something I never thought I'd see race the shadow up the mountain.

Over the years John and I have had a variety of guys join us on our backpacking trips, and some of the times there would be a teenager or two in the group. The teenagers would usually be a family member of one of the guys or possibly a friend of the family. Either way we would occasionally have a teenager or two running around camp making us older guys feel older than we were and definitely less energetic than these young bucks running around. Teenagers do make the trip more interesting, and it's amazing what jokes can be played at a moment's notice.

The Setup

For this particular joke, there was no setup, just a spur of the moment idea and two teenagers who took on the challenge.

The Joke: Let's Chase That Shadow!
Location: Base Camp 1

This particular year, there were two teenagers who were brothers, these were the same teenagers who watched me eat the fake poop on a previous trip. They were a year or two older now, and both were very competitive in many ways and always seemed to have a lot of bottled up energy in them, so much energy it would cause us old-timers to wish these kids would just run off into the woods for an hour or two so we could relax. Their energy reminded me of when I was younger especially when my dad was fed up with me and my brothers running around the house. He would typically yell at us, "Get out of the house and go play on the freeway!" Of course we wouldn't do that, but we would head outside so we wouldn't get in trouble.

One evening at Base Camp 1, just as the sun was starting to set, all the older guys were doing a few things around camp from relaxing, cleaning up after dinner, or just trying to read a book while the two teenagers were running around like two chickens with their heads cut off. Their energy was driving a few of us a bit crazy. Then out of nowhere John comes up with a great idea, an idea which turned out to be a pretty good joke.

John decided to tell the boys about how other guys in the past would race the shadow up the mountain to our east to see if they could get to the top before the shadow did. He said none of the guys who tried to beat the shadow ever made it, but several of them came very close. The funny thing about John's story was I knew he was telling a lie, since I've been on every trip with him before and nobody ever tried to race the shadow to the top of this mountain, or any mountain for that matter, but that didn't stop me from jumping right in and going along with the his story. Plus, I knew it took us a lot longer than an hour to climb this mountain in the past and the shadow would take almost that amount of time to reach the top if these boys were to head out at the very moment John was telling the story. Even though the story John told the boys was a total lie, and nobody in their right mind would attempt climbing the mountain when the sun was going down, I jumped in and said I'd try climbing it again, which of course caused the boys to take on the challenge too.

Soon John, the two boys, and I were off. As soon as the boys got ahead of us, which didn't take more than a minute or two, John and I turned around and went back to camp. As we turned around to head back to camp we yelled to the boys and encouraged them to beat the shadow and become the first to ever reach the top before the shadow did. We told the boys we knew we couldn't do it, but had all the faith in the world that they could.

As the boys were heading to the top, their father asked where his boys were. John told him about the joke he was playing on his boys and that his boys were on their way up the mountain. As a matter of fact, they were almost halfway up the mountain by the time their father knew. When the father heard the news he started to laugh and couldn't believe his boys fell for yet another joke. As we sat there in camp, watching the shadow slowly climb the mountain, the two boys were right on the heels of the shadow line trying to get to the top before it did.

The second half of the boys' journey was a lot steeper than the beginning and the altitude made it a bit harder to breath, but these teenage boys just kept on going and going. We watched these guys climb up some very steep terrain and even lost sight of them a couple of times as they made their assent to the top. To our surprise, the boys actually reached the top of the mountain about a minute or two before the shadow line caught up to them. We could see the boys with our binoculars as they stood high on top of this mountain peak waving their arms and acting like they had climbed Mt. Everest. They actually beat the shadow, but the joke was still in play since now they had to climb back down!

As mentioned earlier, once the shadow hit the top of the mountain, it starts to get dark very quickly in and around camp. With no moon, it made traveling in the dark a bit more hazardous. So what made this joke even better was John didn't tell the boys to bring their flashlights with them. Now the boys had to figure out how to get down the mountain and back to camp in the dark. It took them less than an hour to reach the top, but it took a little over two hours for them to return. When they got back to camp they were a bit tired, a bit scrapped up here and there, and very proud they were the first to ever beat the shadow to the top of the mountain. One thing for sure, the boy's energy was all used up and everyone in camp enjoyed the peaceful night around the campfire. The boys actually went to bed earlier than normal, which surprised us all.

The next morning when the boys woke up, they were a bit sore, but still very proud they were the first to beat the shadow. It was then when John told them they were not only the first to beat the shadow, they were the first to ever attempt such a thing. John told them the story was made up and none of us thought they would even attempt it. The boys couldn't believe they fell for another joke, but they were very proud of their accomplishment, and for me, I was really pleased the joke went the way it did because it slowed the teenagers down enough where everyone could keep up with them for a change when we broke camp and headed to our next destination.

Chapter 12

The Tale of the Mysterious Exploding Rocks

This backpacking adventure was one of the most recent and probably one of my last few trips I've been on for a while now. I know it's one of my last trips where I played any practical jokes, I'm getting too old for this stuff anymore and most of the time the guys who go backpacking with me are friends of mine and almost all of them have heard or been on the receiving end of one of my jokes. So this year I wasn't planning on trying to fool anyone, at least at first!

On this trip I was lucky to have two friends join me, Dave, who is a really talented actor, and one who I've known for several years from a small theater group we volunteered and performed at. The other friend, Larry, was a coworker at the fire department. Larry had been on a trip or two prior to this one, and this time he asked if his son Jim and one of his friends could join. Both Jim and his friend Bob were twenty-one years old, and both of their fathers were coworkers of mine. We all knew each other fairly well. Bob's dad had joined me on a few backing adventures in previous years and he knew his son would have a good time if he went on the trip. Unfortunately both Jim and Bob's dad had told their sons stories of the practical jokes I had played in years past. They told their sons about my fake poop trick, the mysterious voice in the dark trick, and several others, even the message container gag. Basically I didn't stand a chance to play a joke on these guys, so I had a huge challenge in front of me.

It wasn't until the day before we left home when I found a small box with these itty-bitty firecrackers in it that caused me to think that I could pull off one more practical joke. Soon I plotted out a plan, one that makes me laugh every time I tell the story, I call it the "Exploding Rock" joke.

I'm sure many people have heard stories about Indian tribes and their medicine men; medicine men who were extremely talented in utilizing natural items to create miracles before their tribe, or to heal others when needed. As a kid, and throughout my years in school, I read and heard stories about the Native American Indians and how they used rocks and other hard objects to form their tools and weapons they needed to survive. I also heard stories on how their medicine men had the ability to forecast the weather, speak of the future, and do other mysterious things, which gained them respect and a place of honor within their tribe. On this adventure, two unsuspecting young men would learn even more about the Native American Indian medicine man and a lot more about a specific type of rock we had laying around camp.

This rock has now made backpacking history, and it's one any medicine man would have enjoyed having if it really had existed.

The Setup

All that is needed for this joke to work is one hundred very small firecrackers and a person who knows how to tell a story, a story that takes at least three days to tell. By the way, these firecrackers can typically be found at any fireworks stand and are legal in most states.

The Joke: The Tale of the Mysterious Exploding Rocks
Location: This can be played out in most areas where fireworks are allowed. It should not be done in areas where fireworks, especially firecrackers, are banned or illegal.

As I mentioned earlier, on the day before the trip I was going through a few items in my garage deciding what I should pack in my backpack and what I should leave behind. It seemed every year my backpack was getting heavier, and this year was no exception. However, I did need to figure out what items I would need to play a joke on Jim and Bob, the two young men joining us this year. Then, as if I found a lost treasure, right before my eyes I saw this small little box, a box that said, "Take me on your trip." The box was about one inch wide, four inches long, and a half inch thick. The color and lettering on the box was a bit faded, but you could still read the word "firecrackers" on the side of it. I had totally forgotten I had these things in my garage, and instantly I knew what I was going to do with them. I was going to take them with me on this trip no matter what they weighed. Of course they only weighed a few ounces. If I remembered right, these tiny firecrackers were only good for making a small, and I mean small, burst, I wouldn't even call it an explosion. They did however make a nice popping sound, so I knew they would work for the joke. I only had to ask my actor friend, Dave, to help me out with the story and the performance of a lifetime.

While we were on the twelve-hour drive to the trailhead, we stopped to get some fuel for the vehicle and some needed "road trip" food. While I was fueling up the vehicle I was able to call Dave over to the rear of the vehicle and show him the small packet of firecrackers I had in my backpack. I told him of my plan to play a joke on Jim and Bob, but I needed his help. The joke wouldn't be fully played out for a few days from now, but I needed Dave to help me set the guys up while we were driving along and continue to work on the story as we were hiking along the trail and even once we're in camp. I needed him to not tell them the story, but to tell me the story in hopes they would hear us talking. I needed Jim and Bob to think the story he was telling me was the first time I had ever heard it so the guys would think I was learning something for the first time. The story he needed to develop was one about exploding rocks and how medicine men once used them to show their tribe they had magical powers or whatever he wanted to add to the story.

I then explained to Dave the story I thought up and told him he had free reign to take the ball and run with it. The following is the story I told Dave hoping he would ponder upon it and use his acting skills to ask the right questions and to sell the story to others who would over hear him as he told the story, or asked questions of me.

I told Dave about a fictitious rock that when soaked it in a pot of water for a given amount of time, the water will slowly seep into the stone saturating it to a point where it actually allows the water to seep into small air pockets within the stone itself. Once the inner air pockets are filled with water, the stone actually swells up, or creates a seal around the water encapsulating the water, so it does not leak out of the stone after the rock is removed from the pot of water.

My story is how the Indian medicine men would soak these types of rocks prior to a ceremony or gathering with their tribe and then place a few of these rocks into the middle of their fires. Since water expands when heated, the rocks would explode apart causing everyone to believe the medicine man had these extraordinary powers.

What I needed Dave to do was act as if he had a vast amount of knowledge of the lifestyles of the northwest American Indians and how they lived off the land. I also need him to act as if he was only telling me about his knowledge and not to strike up a conversation with Jim and Bob unless they specifically came to him and asked for more information.

Now that Dave knew what I needed him to do and he had full knowledge I had a box of about one hundred firecrackers, the joke was officially on and Jim and Bob hopefully wouldn't be suspicious at all, but enjoy the ride they were about to go on.

Once our tank was full and the munchies for the road trip were on board, we headed off to our destination, which was about another ten hours away. I was driving and Dave was in the front passenger seat when after about an hour or two Dave out of the blue said, "Hey, Dennis, do you know much about the American Indians who once lived in the area we are going to?" I of course said no, to which he replied, "Well, I've been reading this really good book about the northwest American Indians and how they lived off the land, and how they utilized almost everything they could find to build their dwellings, obtain their food sources, and even how they made medicine from different herbs. It's a really cool book." He went on to tell a few stories from this imaginary book, but none of it related to anything about exploding rocks but had everything in setting up a foundation when the time came. We knew Jim and Bob were hearing everything since they were in the back seat of my vehicle and Dave spoke loud enough to engage in a conversation with Jim's dad, Larry, who was also in the back seat. This conversation went on for about a half hour or so before we started talking about other things like when lunch is and where our next stop is.

After a few more hours, specifically when we passed an area where there was a lot of volcanic rock in the area, Dave struck up another conversation about the book he was reading. He asked me if I knew anything about the rock in the area where we were going, and I said, "Nope, not really." At this point he went into a story or two on how these Indians would use a variety of stones for key elements in their lifestyle, he told me how they used smooth rocks to mash their flower from the grains they would harvest in the spring and summer months, the rocks they would use to form their arrowheads, and even rocks they would use to build fire rings or pits that would fit within their dwellings. Once again he did not mention anything about rocks that would explode or anything about Indian medicine men. He just kept on building his story and gaining more interest from Jim and Bob. As we drove on, and even into the first two days of our backpacking trip, Dave would bring up little stories about his knowledge of the northwestern American Indians, and each time he would make sure Jim and Bob were in earshot so they too would also hear his stories.

One day, I believe it was our second day in the back country, Dave and I were fishing along the edge of a really nice lake. I was about fifteen feet away from Dave in one direction and Jim and Bob were about twenty feet away in the opposite direction just sitting along the shoreline relaxing. Knowing where Jim and Bob were, Dave and I planned to set the hook and prepare for the evening's events. Dave, in a loud voice, asked me about a specific type of rock, a rock he thought he saw near our camp and he thought this type of rock was used by the Native American Indians, specifically by their medicine men. Dave's loud voice carried very well, which made it very easy for Jim and Bob to hear what was being discussed between Dave and me.

I asked Dave what the rock's name was, and he said it was something like "bass-salt," a name I never heard of and one I believe he made up. Anyway, I said I never heard of bass-salt and had no idea if it existed in the area. Dave said he was sure it was in the area and almost 100 percent sure it was near our camp. I asked Dave if he could explain the shape or the color of the rock and why the medicine men used such a rock. What was funny was that Dave explained the color, size, and shape of a rock that could be found anywhere, but he was doing his best acting when he explained how the medicine men would use this rock to show off their powers and to gain higher respect from the elders of the tribe. He was so on point with his description and what appeared to be a knowledge of the American Indians that I almost believed what he was saying, and I was in on the joke.

As he and I were talking, or almost yelling back and forth to each other, I could see Jim and Bob paying a lot more attention than before, I believe they even moved a few feet closer to Dave so they could hear him better. Now that I saw these guys listening to almost every word Dave and I were saying, I asked Dave to explain to me how this rock was used by the medicine men. Dave then explained in almost expert detail how the rocks would react when they were soaked in water and then placed in the coals of the fire pits. He said he read the medicine men knew how long it would take for the rock to burst depending on the size and shape of the stone. They could then set the rocks in the fire, say a specific spell or incantation, then poof, the rock would explode and everyone around the fire would be amazed at their abilities. Once Dave told me this, I told him that it made sense I knew firsthand how concrete does the same thing. Dave knew I was a firefighter, so it made it easy for me to relate to him I had witnessed small portions of concrete floors and some masonry walls burst or breakaway once cool water had impacted their super-heated surfaces. That's probably how these rocks react as well.

As we sat there along the banks of the lake not catching a single fish, but landing two unsuspecting gullible backpackers, Dave and I kept on talking. Dave was awesome, he spent the next twenty minutes or more explaining all sorts of (made-up) facts about the rock and how it was used. He also went on to tell other stories that had nothing to do with the rock, but made the entire story that much more believable. Soon I knew Jim and Bob were on the hook and ready to be played.

As the day grew into evening, I started to get dinner ready for the group. As I started to cook dinner Dave reached over to an empty can we found earlier in the day. The can was an old coffee can some other group or backpacker left behind and one we decided to pick up and hike it out with our trash. (I hate finding other people's garbage. If you pack it in, pack it out!). Sorry, back to the story.

As I started to prepare dinner, Dave, without making a production, went about his business and filled up the old coffee can with water and placed a few rocks into it. He didn't say anything, he didn't show anyone what he was doing, he just casually placed these innocent rocks into a can of water. As he did this, I only asked few simple words, "Do you think those are the same kind of rocks?" Dave just nodded his head and said, "I think they are." Of course both Dave and I knew Jim and Bob were within feet of us and saw what Dave had done and what we had said, so we knew they were paying close attention to those few rocks in the can of water.

After dinner everyone was sitting around the campfire talking about what we did that day and listening to Dave and Jim play their guitars they carried in on their backpacks. The rest of us were kicking back enjoying the evening, the music, and the beautiful night air. As the fire was glowing I would stoke it occasionally and frequently toss in a few little pine cones, which were laying around our camp. Not only did I toss in an occasional pine cone, Jim's dad, Larry, was also tossing his fair share of mini pine cones into the fire. As we were relaxing, tossing pine cones into the fire, Dave got up and went over to the coffee can he had filled with water earlier and where he had placed a few rocks in it to soak. As Dave got the rocks out, I again asked him, "So do you think these rocks are the same kind of rocks you told me about?" Again, he said he thought they were, and as he tossed them into the nice hot coals of the fire, he explained to Larry what he told me earlier that day. The only question I had for Dave was, "How many rocks did you toss in there and how long do you think it will take if it works?" Dave said he tossed in about four rocks and it shouldn't be long.

With the knowledge of four rocks being tossed in and it shouldn't take long being said, I took four little pine cones, stuck in a small little firecracker in each pine cone, tossed them in the fire and waited for them to explode. Sure enough within seconds they popped and to the surprise of everyone, the exploding rocks Dave had found worked. Jim and Bob quickly jumped to their feet and asked Dave where he found these rocks and if he would show them where they could get more. Within minutes, Jim, Bob, and Dave were off heading out into the dark looking for more exploding rocks. As they were out of the camp looking for more rocks, I explained to Larry what I was doing and got him to help me out with the joke. I handed Larry several firecrackers and told him to do the same thing I had done with the small pine cones once he knew how many rocks Jim and Bob tossed into the fire.

Soon Dave was back in camp, but there was no sign of Jim or Bob. We asked where they were and Dave just said, "I left them out there scavenging for rocks, they should be back soon." We all wondered how many rocks they would bring back, and Larry couldn't believe his son had fallen for this gag. I predicted Jim and Bob would return with their shirts untucked and held out in front of them as if they were carrying a bunch of eggs they just got from a hen house. I figured they would bring back at least fifty rocks if not more. Both Dave and Larry said they doubted it, but about twenty minutes later, Jim and Bob showed up with more rocks in their untucked shirts than anyone could count. The two quickly placed handfuls of these rocks in the coffee can where the water overflowed because of so many rocks being placed in it. Jim and Bob then eagerly awaited the proper soaking time, which Dave made up, and soon they were ready to place a few of these rocks into the hot coals of the fire. As they did, either Larry, Dave, or I would ask how many they tossed in, and sure enough, that's how many pine cones with a firecracker neatly secured to it got tossed in the fire. Soon the pop sound would take place and soon more rocks were being tossed into the fire pit. It was amazing to see the mysterious exploding rocks transpire in front of our eyes.

After about an hour or more of rock after rock being tossed into the fire pit, we were starting to run out of firecrackers and Jim and Bob were now out of rocks. We thought the two had enough, but nope, they ran back out into the darkness to gather even more rocks. While they were away from camp, Larry, Dave, and I discussed how we would spoil Jim and Bob's fun by telling them the truth. I had an idea on what to do, so we all agreed I would be the one telling them they had been had. Larry also reminded me that he and Bob's dad told them to watch out for me and my practical jokes, so by me telling them they had been had, it would be even better than Dave telling them they were had. Jim and Bob obviously didn't listen to their fathers and they sure didn't think Dave would be involved with a joke, so it was time to end it with one last bang!

As the two returned to camp, they actually brought back a huge rock to see if it would do the same as the smaller rocks, but make a bigger explosion. I frowned against it, and so did Dave and Larry. However, this didn't stop them from soaking more rocks in the coffee can and continue tossing them into the fire until Dave and Larry were out of firecrackers and I was down to my last one. As I reached my final firecracker, Jim and Bob placed a fairly large pile of rocks in the fire pit at one time to see if they could get a bigger reaction. As they did I said we better all move back and see what happens. After about five minutes of nothing happening, I decided to approach the fire pit. Larry told me to be careful and so did Dave, but Jim and Bob just watched hoping the rocks would soon explode and scare the living daylights out of me.

As I approached the fire pit, I grabbed a stick to poke at the wood, which was laying over the hot coals, and several rocks, which had been tossed into the fire pit. I poked at the fire as if I was looking for the reason why the last batch of rocks didn't explode. As I pretended to poke around, I told the group I thought I found out what the problem was. Everyone said, "What was it?" I asked Jim and Bob to join me by the fire pit and to look at the coals I was looking at. The three of us were all bent over, hands on our knees, faces looking deep into the coals of the fire pit as if our heads were all attached on the same set of shoulders. Our faces were glowing from the embers in the fire pit as I reached out and pointed to the coals. In a very somber voice I asked Jim and Bob, "Do you see why the rocks aren't exploding?" To which they replied, "No, why aren't they?"

As they asked this question, I reached into my pocket and with all three of us still bent over looking deep into the coals I held out the firecracker and said, "It's because you need one of these to make it work." As Jim's and Bob's eyes focused now on what was in my hand, and not at the coals of the fire, they both saw the tiny little firecracker and realized they had been had. They both jumped back and started laughing at themselves for believing Dave and me. They even said they were both told to watch out for me and my practical jokes and couldn't believe they fell for our story hook, line, and sinker. I think everyone that night laughed for hours about the exploding rocks and how well Dave told his stories and got them all to believe in the northwest American Indian medicine man and his mystical and magical powers and, more importantly, the "Exploding Rocks."

Prior to going to bed that night I could hear Jim and Bob in their tents laughing about the joke which was played on them; they couldn't believe that even though they we're twenty-one years old they still fell for such a stupid trick as exploding rocks. "What were we thinking?" was one of the things I remember them asking themselves as we all fell asleep that night. Then right before I fell asleep, they yelled out to the rest of us, "Hey, you guys aren't going to tell anyone back home about this, are you?" To which we all said in a devious voice, "Sure we won't, you can trust us."

The next couple of days, and even during the long drive home, we all had fun discussing the exploding rocks and how funny it was. What Jim didn't know was that I knew he was going to have lunch with a mutual friend of ours a couple of days after we got home. Prior to the lunch date, I contacted our friend and told him about the joke I played on Jim. I then asked him if he would play a joke on Jim while at lunch. He said he would love to, so I suggested he bring a couple of small rocks with him to lunch and sometime during lunch take the rocks out of his pocket and drop them in his glass of water, then say to Jim, "I heard if you soak these rocks in water and then toss them into a fire, they would explode. Have you heard of such a thing?" Our friend did this, and Jim couldn't believe he was being played again, by someone who wasn't even on the trip. It was another amazing day for Jim.

Jim and Bob were great sports, and to this day when I see them we have fun reliving that trip and talking about the fun we all had, exploding rocks and all.

Next time everyone is sitting around a campfire and something makes a loud popping noise in the fire pit, remember the exploding rock story and have fun with telling it again and again. It's one of my favorite jokes while out in the woods.

Chapter 13

The Story of "Falling Rock"

As I wrote this book, my two daughters, who are now grown and have families of their own, reminded me of a story I told them when they were little girls riding in the back seat of our SUV while on a camping trip.

While driving along a mountain highway with my wife and our two daughters, I saw a sign posted alongside the road as we approached a rocky area ahead. The sign read, "Watch for Falling Rock." With this sign in mind I asked my daughters, who were about five and eight years old, if they saw the sign. Of course they said no, they were too busy playing one of their videogames or reading a book.

I told them I would keep an eye out for another sign like it and would make sure they saw it the next time we drove by one. Sure enough, a mile further down the road there was another sign asking drivers to "watch for falling rock." As we drove closer to the sign, I pointed it out to my daughters and told them the following story. This story kept them looking out the window for miles while on this trip and other trips as they grew older. The story I told them goes as follows:

> Back in the early days, the American Indians named their sons and daughters after things they would see once their children were born. Some of the names were Flying Eagle, Running Bear, Soaring Hawk, or things of this nature. The sign

we saw was about one of the most mysterious Native Americans, Falling Rock.

Falling Rock was the son of one of the greatest Indian chiefs. It is believed the day his son was born a great earthquake shook their village causing a huge rock to fall from a nearby mountain top. At the same time the huge rock fell, the chief's son was born. The rock was so huge it shook the ground, and the great chief knew he had to name his son "Falling Rock."

When "Falling Rock" was a very young boy, he was smart and very strong and not like other children of his age, he was allowed to go on a hunting expedition with his father and other men from the tribe. While out hunting it was believed Falling Rock was tracking a herd of deer when he got lost and his tribe could not find him. His tribe looked for days and days to find him, but Falling Rock was never found again. The tribe knew he wasn't eaten by bears or by other wild animals because they would often find signs or footprints of him but could never find him. It was a mystery to them how the young boy disappeared and how they could never track him down.

The "Watch for Falling Rock" signs we see along the road today or other signs with just his name "Falling Rock" are tributes to the son of the great Indian chief who was lost several years ago. People often see glimpses of Falling Rock in the mountains and valleys throughout this great nation, and it is up to us to always keep an eye out for him.

In addition, I said the signs we see with pictures of a deer on them are also there to remind us of what Falling Rock was hunting the day he got lost. The deer signs are possibly signs where Falling Rock was tracking the deer and where we need to keep an eye out for any signs of deer and possibly Falling Rock in the area.

After I told the story, my daughters would almost always point out the signs along the road and ask if I saw them and wondered if they would see the spirit of the lost Indian boy or possibly the deer he was tracking. This went on for years, and to my surprise, they still remember the story.

Both my daughters are older now and have families of their own. My wife and I have been blessed with grandchildren who are almost about the age to tell this story to again. I'm sure either I or my daughters will tell their children the story in hopes their kids will be looking out the windows for the lost Indian boy, "Falling Rock," while at the same time taking in all the beautiful scenery and landscapes God has placed before us to admire and enjoy.

I hope this story is something other parents will tell their kids while driving down the road, especially when they want their kids to stop playing videogames or watching movies in the car, but instead hope their children will take the time to look out the windows and take in the amazing views of the wonderful world we live in.

About the Author

Well over thirty-seven years ago, Dennis started backpacking and enjoying the outdoors more than most people will ever do. Since the first time he ever put on a backpack to now, he has hiked all over the Sierra Nevada mountain range in northern California; hiked several parts of Arizona, mostly in and around the Grand Canyon; climbed a few mountains in Colorado, Utah, and Nevada, all while enjoying God's country and time with his friends and family.

Over the years, Dennis has introduced several of his friends and family members to the great outdoors. In addition, he has had the opportunity to play innocent practical jokes on them too, all of whom have trusted him to protect them while out in the wilderness and to bring them home safe again. He too has had practical jokes played on him, so he thought it would be fun to share some of his most memorable practical jokes within this book in hopes they will bring a smile to your face and inspire you to replicate or improve upon the jokes for your own enjoyment.

Dennis was a firefighter for over thirty-seven years. He worked his way up from a rookie firefighter to the fire chief over these years, and in doing so he found firefighters to be really good at playing practical jokes on each other, which explains where he came up with several of his ideas to get back at his fellow firefighter friends who he would take backpacking.

CPSIA information can be obtained
at www.ICGtesting.com
Printed in the USA
LVHW040727261119
638496LV00004B/424/P

9 781645 311867